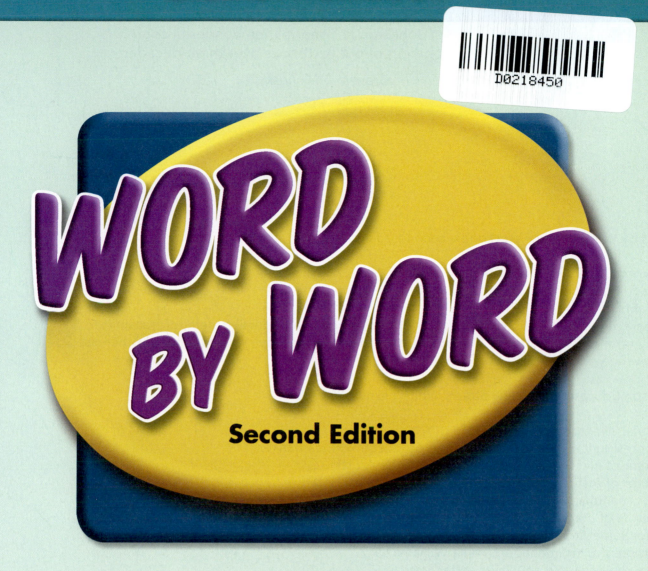

WORD BY WORD

Second Edition

Steven J. Molinsky • Bill Bliss

Contributing Authors
Dorothy Almanza
Deborah L. Schaffer
Carol H. Van Duzer

Illustrated by
Richard E. Hill

PEARSON
Longman

Dedicated to Janet Johnston in honor of her wonderful contribution
to the development of our textbooks over three decades.

Steven J. Molinsky
Bill Bliss

Word by Word Literacy Workbook, second edition

Copyright © 2009 by Prentice Hall Regents
Pearson Education, Inc.

Pearson Education, 10 Bank Street, White Plains, NY 10606

Editorial director: Pam Fishman
Vice president, director of design and production: Rhea Banker
Director of electronic production: Aliza Greenblatt
Director of manufacturing: Patrice Fraccio
Senior manufacturing manager: Edith Pullman
Directors of marketing: Oliva Fernandez, Carol Brown
Production editor: Diane Cipollone
Associate paging manager: Paula Williams
Senior digital layout specialist: Lisa Ghiozzi
Text design: Wendy Wolf
Cover design: Tracey Munz Cataldo, Warren Fischbach
Realia creation: Paula Williams
Illustrations: Richard E. Hill

ISBN 0-13-189228-2
ISBN 978-0-13189228-6
Pearson Longman on the Web
PearsonLongman.com offers online resources for teachers and students. Access our
Companion Websites, our online catalog, and our local offices around the world.

Visit us at pearsonlongman.com.

Printed in the United States of America
1 2 3 4 5 6 7 8 9 10 – RRD – 12 11 10 09 08

iv

A CIRCLE THE SAME WORD

1. NAME	STREET	NUMBER	(NAME)	STATE
2. CITY	STATE	ADDRESS	CITY	LAST
3. STATE	STREET	FIRST	LAST	STATE
4. STREET	FIRST	STATE	STREET	LAST
5. ADDRESS	ADDRESS	NAME	NUMBER	CITY

B MATCHING

1. STATE — GARDEN STREET

2. ZIP CODE — 227-93-6185

3. STREET — GLORIA SANCHEZ

4. TELEPHONE NUMBER — CA

5. NAME — 323-524-3278

6. SOCIAL SECURITY NUMBER — 90036

A B C D E F G H I J K L M N O P Q R

C FILL OUT THE FORM

NAME: _____
FIRST   LAST

ADDRESS: _____
NUMBER   STREET   APT.

_____
CITY   STATE   ZIP CODE

TELEPHONE NUMBER: _____

SOCIAL SECURITY NUMBER: _____

D FILL OUT THE FORM

NAME
FIRST   LAST

ADDRESS
NUMBER   STREET   APT.

CITY   STATE   ZIP CODE

TELEPHONE NUMBER

SOCIAL SECURITY NUMBER

S T U V W X Y Z 0 1 2 3 4 5 6 7 8 9

E INTERVIEW

Talk to three people.   Write the information.

Name	Telephone Number
1. _____	_____
2. _____	_____
3. _____	_____

F LISTENING

Listen and circle the words you hear.

1. (name)
   address

2. zip code
   apartment number

3. telephone
   social security

4. state
   street

5. middle
   city

6. first
   last

G JOURNAL

My first name is _____.

My last name is _____.

My address is _____.

My telephone number is _____.

A WHO ARE THEY?

1. grandmother   <u>b</u>

2. father   ___

3. son   ___

4. daughter   ___

5. mother   ___

6. grandfather   ___

B MATCHING

1. FATHER

2. SISTER

3. BROTHER

4. MOTHER

5. SON

6. DAUGHTER

sister

mother

daughter

 father

brother

son

Aa Bb Cc Dd Ee Ff Gg Hh Ii Jj Kk Ll Mm

1. w i fe

   s _ ster

2. fathe _

   mothe _

3. hu _ band

   _ on

4. grands _ n

   br _ ther

5. b _ by

   d _ ughter

6. grandmo _ _ er

   grandfa _ _ er

D WHICH GROUP?

brother	father	mother	son
daughter	husband	sister	wife

Parents

Children

1. f a t h e r

2. m _ _ _ _ _

3. h _ _ _ _ _ _

4. w _ _ _

5. s _ _

6. d _ _ _ _ _ _ _

7. b _ _ _ _ _ _

8. s _ _ _ _ _

Nn Oo Pp Qq Rr Ss Tt Uu Vv Ww Xx Yy Zz

A WHO ARE THEY?

1. nephew   <u>d</u>

2. aunt   ___

3. niece   ___

4. cousin   ___

5. uncle   ___

B WHAT'S MISSING?

1. a <u>u</u> n t

   _ n c l e

2. _ e p h e w

   _ i e c e

3. c o u s i _

   u _ c l e

4. _ o n – i n – l a w

   _ i s t e r – i n – l a w

5. m o _ _ e r – i n – l a w

   f a _ _ e r – i n – l a w

6. s i s t _ _ – i n – l a w

   b _ o t h _ _ – i n – l a w

C WHICH GROUP?

| aunt | cousin | nephew | niece | uncle |

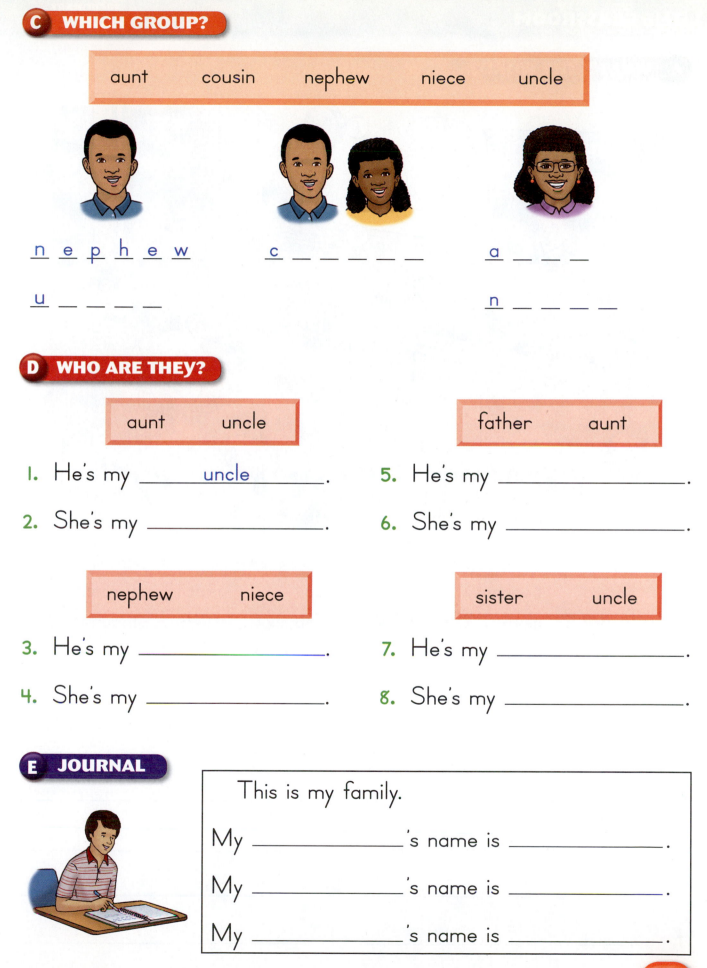

n e p h e w   c _ _ _ _ _   a _ _ _

u _ _ _ _   n _ _ _ _

D WHO ARE THEY?

| aunt | uncle |

1. He's my _____uncle_____ .

2. She's my _____ .

| nephew | niece |

3. He's my _____ .

4. She's my _____ .

| father | aunt |

5. He's my _____ .

6. She's my _____ .

| sister | uncle |

7. He's my _____ .

8. She's my _____ .

E JOURNAL

This is my family.

My _____'s name is _____ .

My _____'s name is _____ .

My _____'s name is _____ .

A   WHAT'S THE WORD?

board	bookcase	desk	map	pencil	student
book	clock	globe	notebook	ruler	teacher

a. _____map_____

b. _____

c. _____

d. _____

e. _____

f. _____

g. _____

h. _____

i. _____

j. _____

k. _____

l. _____

Listen and circle the word you hear.

1. pen   (pencil)   4. eraser   ruler

2. pencil   paper   5. notebook   textbook

3. chalk   clock   6. computer   calculator

C **WHAT'S IN THE CLASSROOM?**

Look at page 4 of the dictionary. Write the correct word.

| book | computer | globe | map | wastebasket |

1. There's a g _ _ _ _ on the bookcase.

2. There's a m _ _ next to the board.

3. There's a b _ _ _ on the teacher's desk.

4. There's a c _ _ _ _ _ _ _ on the table.

5. There's a w _ _ _ _ _ _ _ _ _ _ next to
   the teacher's desk.

D **JOURNAL**

In my classroom there is _____

_____

_____.

A LISTENING

Listen. Put a check under the correct picture.

1. ____✓____ _____   2. _____ _____

3. _____ _____   4. _____ _____

5. _____ _____   6. _____ _____

B MATCHING

1. Open   your name.

2. Write   down.

3. Stand   your book.

4. Sit   the board.

5. Go to   up.

WHAT'S THE ACTION?

Circle	Do	Raise	Work
Close	Go	Turn off	Write

1. _Write_ your name.

2. _____ your book.

3. _____ your hand.

4. _____ to the board.

5. _____ your homework.

6. _____ the answer.

7. _____ in a group.

8. _____ the lights.

A CHOOSE THE CORRECT ANSWER

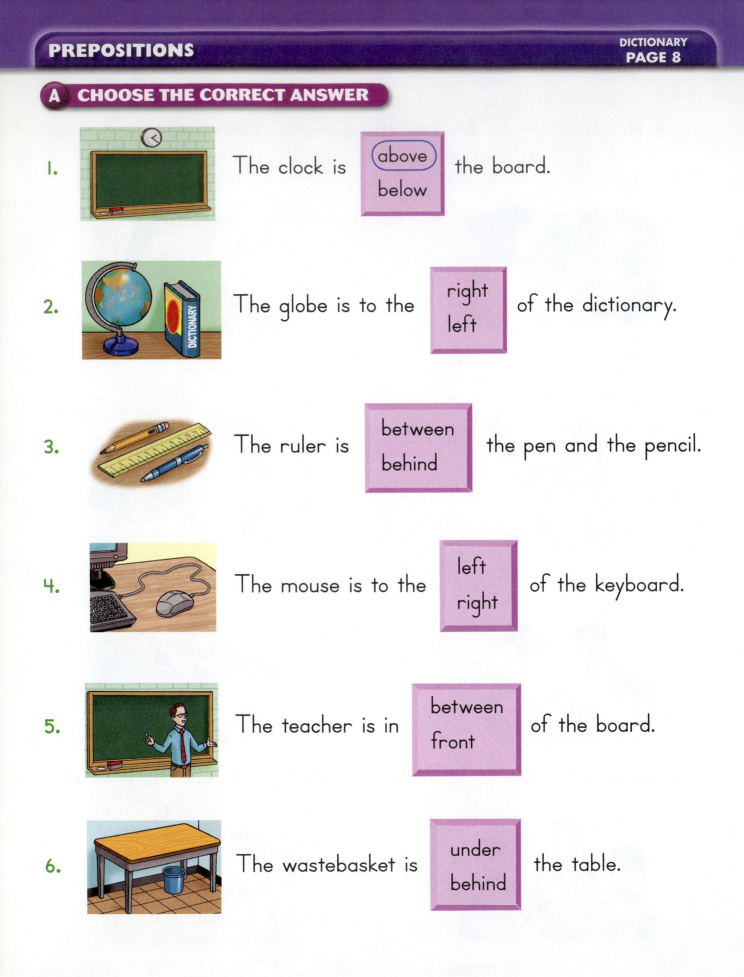

1. The clock is (above) / below the board.

2. The globe is to the right / left of the dictionary.

3. The ruler is between / behind the pen and the pencil.

4. The mouse is to the left / right of the keyboard.

5. The teacher is in between / front of the board.

6. The wastebasket is under / behind the table.

above	in front of	on	under
behind	next to	right	

1. The clock is _____*above*_____ the board.

2. The computer is _____ the table.

3. The map is _____ the bulletin board.

4. The bookcase is _____ the table.

5. The wastebasket is _____ the table.

6. The bulletin board is _____ the map.

7. The globe is to the _____ of the computer.

A   MATCHING

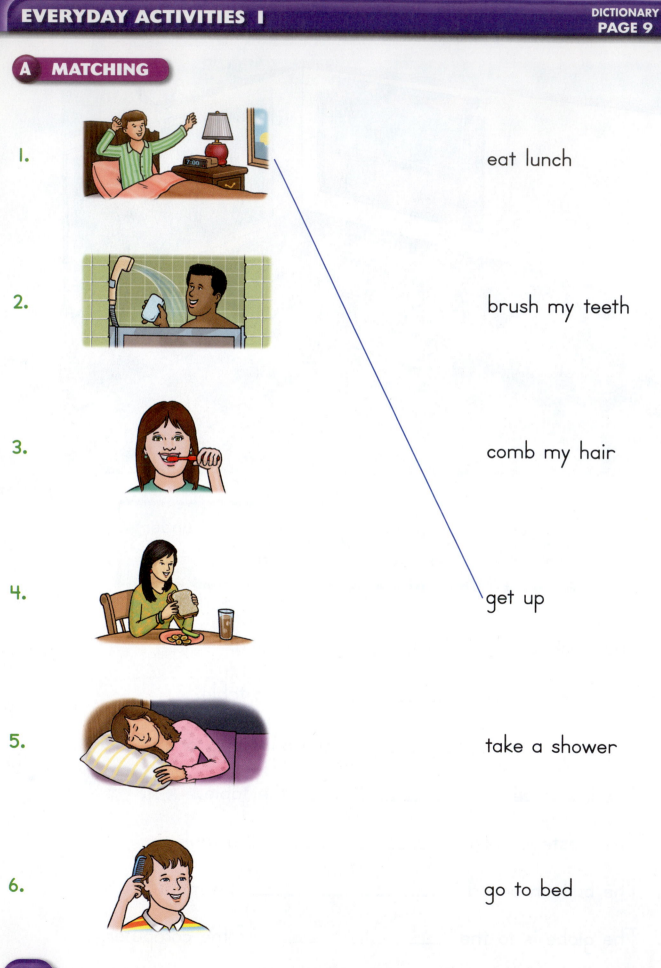

1.

2.

3.

4.

5.

6.

eat lunch

brush my teeth

comb my hair

get up

take a shower

go to bed

B WHAT DO YOU DO EVERY DAY?

| brush | eat | make | shave | sleep | wash |

1. I ___wash___ my face.

2. I _____ breakfast.

3. I _____ .

4. I _____ my hair.

5. I _____ dinner.

6. I _____ .

C LISTENING

Listen. Write the correct number.

___ take a shower   ___ make dinner

___ brush teeth   ___ shave

_1_ take a bath

A LISTENING

Listen. Put a check under the correct picture.

1. __✓__   _____   2. _____   _____

3. _____   _____   4. _____   _____

5. _____   _____   6. _____   _____

B MATCHING

1. feed   home

2. go to   the dishes

3. wash   the cat

4. come   work

C WHAT DO YOU DO EVERY DAY?

clean	drive	iron	study	work

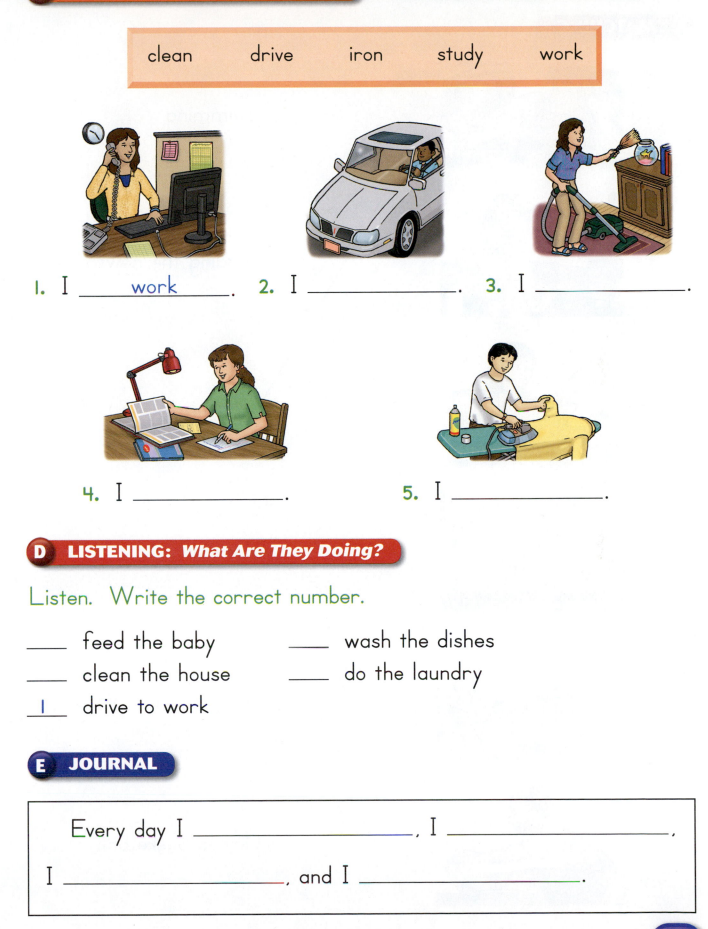

1. I _____work_____. 2. I _____. 3. I _____.

4. I _____. 5. I _____.

D LISTENING: *What Are They Doing?*

Listen. Write the correct number.

____ feed the baby   ____ wash the dishes

____ clean the house   ____ do the laundry

_1_ drive to work

E JOURNAL

Every day I _____, I _____,

I _____, and I _____.

A MATCHING

1.

   swimming

2.

   reading the newspaper

3.

   listening to the radio

4.

   exercising

5.

   practicing the piano

6.

   playing basketball

listening   planting   playing   reading   watching   writing

1. I'm _____watching_____ TV.

2. I'm _____ the guitar.

3. I'm _____ flowers.

4. I'm _____ a letter.

5. I'm _____ a book.

6. I'm _____ to music.

C **LISTENING:** *What Are They Doing?*

Listen. Write the correct number.

____ exercising

____ swimming

____ using the computer

__1__ playing the piano

____ playing basketball

____ playing the guitar

A WHAT'S THE WORD?

afternoon	morning	new	night	soon	thanks

1. Good **m o r n i n g**.

2. Good _____.

3. How are you? Fine, _____.

4. What's ____? Not much.

5. See you _____.

6. Good _____.

B MATCHING

1. Good   new?
2. How are   later.
3. Fine,   you?
4. What's   afternoon.
5. See you   thanks.

| Hello | Hi | introduce | meet | speak | sorry |

1. **H e l l o .** My name is Marco.

   _ _ . I'm Mohamed.

   Welcome Students

2. May I please _ _ _ _ _ _ to Amber?

   I'm _ _ _ _ _ _ . She isn't here right now.

3. I'd like to _ _ _ _ _ _ _ _ my mother.

   Nice to _ _ _ _ you.

1. I don't   me.
2. Excuse   repeat that?
3. Thank   understand.
4. Can you please   a question?
5. May I ask   you.

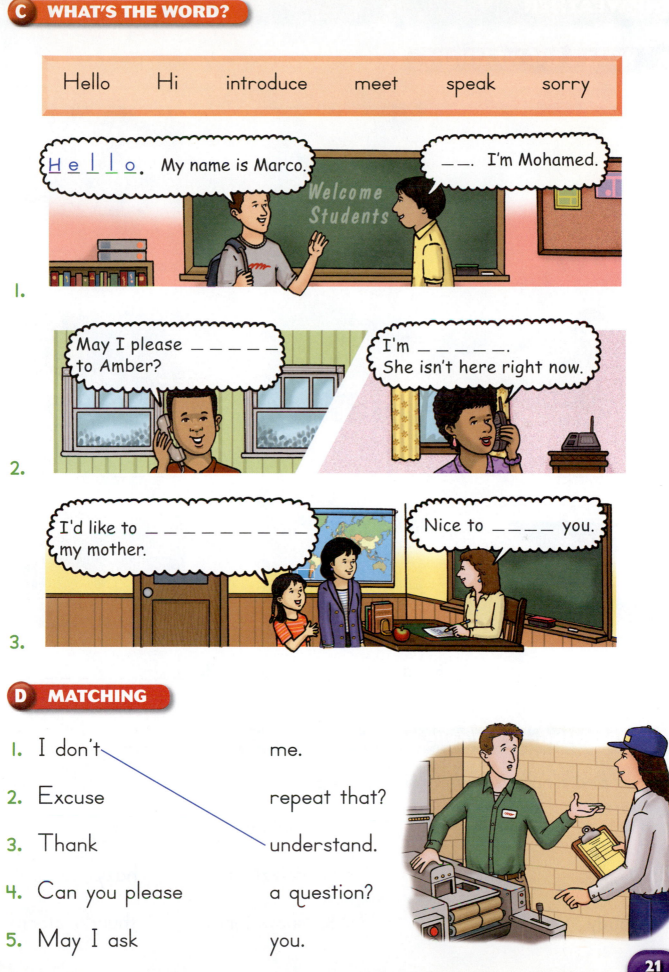

A WHAT'S THE WEATHER?

1. s u n n y

2. c _ _ _ _ _ _

3. r _ _ _ _ _ _ _

4. h _ _ _ _

5. f _ _ _ _

6. s _ _ _ _ _ _ _

7. w _ _ _ _

8. s _ _ _ _ _ _

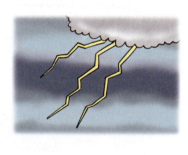

9. l _ _ _ _ _ _ _ _ _

B LISTENING: *What's the Weather Forecast?*

Listen and circle the weather you hear.

1.	sunny	(snowing)	4. muggy	foggy
2.	windy	humid	5. drizzling	hazy
3.	cloudy	clear	6. snowstorm	thunderstorm

| cold | cool | freezing | hot | warm |

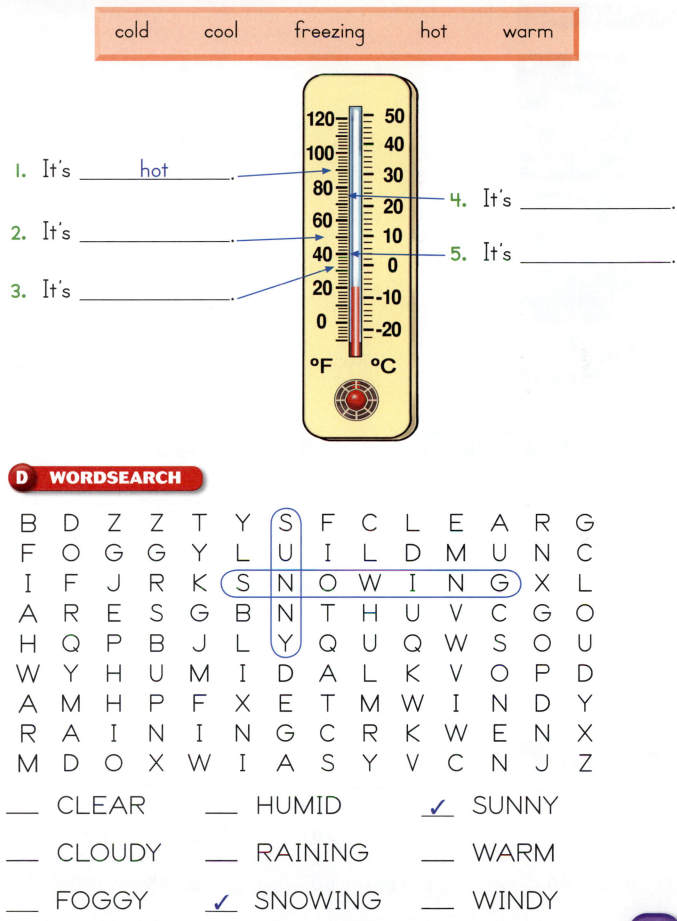

1. It's _____hot_____.

2. It's _____.

3. It's _____.

4. It's _____.

5. It's _____.

D WORDSEARCH

```
B  D  Z  Z  T  Y  S  F  C  L  E  A  R  G
F  O  G  G  Y  L  U  I  L  D  M  U  N  C
I  F  J  R  K  S  N  O  W  I  N  G  X  L
A  R  E  S  G  B  N  T  H  U  V  C  G  O
H  Q  P  B  J  L  Y  Q  U  Q  W  S  O  U
W  Y  H  U  M  I  D  A  L  K  V  O  P  D
A  M  H  P  F  X  E  T  M  W  I  N  D  Y
R  A  I  N  I  N  G  C  R  K  W  E  N  X
M  D  O  X  W  I  A  S  Y  V  C  N  J  Z
```

___ CLEAR   ___ HUMID   ✔ SUNNY

___ CLOUDY   ___ RAINING   ___ WARM

___ FOGGY   ✔ SNOWING   ___ WINDY

A MATCHING

1. [domino]
2. [domino]
3. [domino]
4. [domino]
5. [domino]

five   5

three   7

six   8

eight   3

seven   6

B WHAT'S THE NUMBER?

1. nine   _____9_____
2. four   _____
3. sixteen   _____
4. twelve   _____
5. fifty   _____

C WHAT'S THE WORD?

4   _____four_____

6   _____

13   _____

70   _____

100   _____

D LISTENING

Listen and circle the number you hear.

1. (13) 30   3. 17 70   5. 42 24

2. 14 40   4. 16 60   6. 35 53

MATCHING

1. third — 9th
2. ninth — 60th
3. first — 12th
4. twelfth — 3rd
5. sixtieth — 1st

6. eleventh — 80th
7. eighth — 11th
8. fourth — 14th
9. eightieth — 4th
10. fourteenth — 8th

F **WHAT'S THE NUMBER?**

1. second ___2nd___
2. tenth _____
3. thirteenth _____
4. first _____
5. fiftieth _____
6. third _____

G **WHAT'S THE WORD?**

14th ___fourteenth___

6th _____

60th _____

11th _____

20th _____

21st _____

H **MATCHING**

1. four — fifth
2. five — second
3. two — fourth
4. one — third
5. three — tenth
6. ten — first

I **LISTENING**

Listen and circle the number you hear.

1. 4th (14th) 40th
2. 7th 17th 70th
3. 3rd 13th 30th
4. 8th 18th 80th
5. 2nd 22nd 32nd

A WHAT TIME IS IT?

10:00 _____   _____   _____

 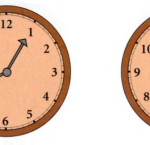  

_____   _____   _____   _____

B CHOOSE THE CORRECT ANSWER

1. a. It's a quarter to three.
   b. It's a quarter to four.

2. a. It's seven thirty.
   b. It's six thirty.

3. a. It's five thirty.
   b. It's six twenty-five.

4. a. It's a quarter to eight.
   b. It's a quarter after eight.

C MATCHING

1. a quarter to six	6:30	ten to seven
2. six twenty	6:15	five forty-five
3. half past six	5:45	six thirty
4. a quarter after six	6:50	twenty after six
5. six fifty	6:20	six fifteen

D CHOOSE THE CORRECT TIME

1. (7:00 A.M.)   2. noon   3. noon   4. 10:00 A.M.
   7:00 P.M.   midnight   midnight   10:00 P.M.

E LISTENING

Listen and circle the time you hear.

1. 2:30   (8:30)   4. 5:45   6:45

2. 10:00   2:00   5. 1:30   2:30

3. 3:15   4:15   6. 5:01   1:05

F JOURNAL: *My Daily Schedule*

I get up at _____. I eat breakfast at _____.
I go to school at _____. I have lunch at _____.
I eat dinner at _____. I go to sleep at _____.

A WHAT IS IT?

1. __p e n n y__

   __1¢__   __$.01__

2. _ _ _ _

   ___ ___

3. _ _ _ _ _ _ _

   ___ ___

4. _ _ _ _ _ _

   ___ ___

5. _ _ _ _ _ _ _ _ _

   ___ ___

B WHAT'S THE AMOUNT?

| $.05 | $.12 | $.15 | $.25 | $.26 | $.40 | $.75 | $1.00 |

1. __$.05__

2. _____

3. _____

4. _____

5. _____

6. _____

7. _____

8. _____

1. 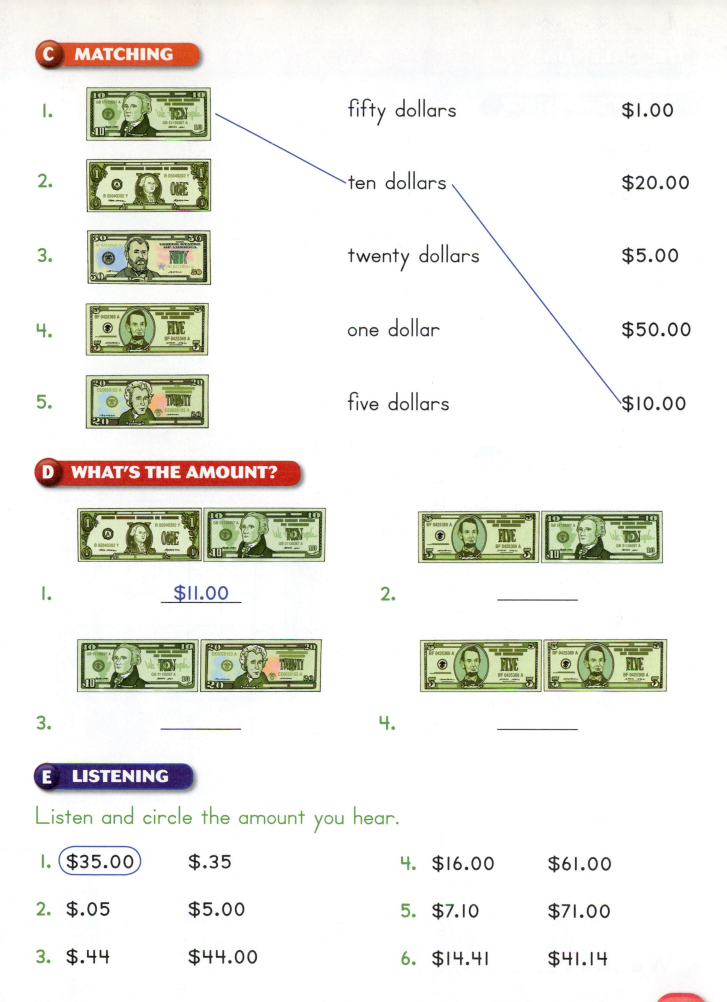 fifty dollars $1.00

2.   ten dollars $20.00

3.   twenty dollars $5.00

4.   one dollar $50.00

5.   five dollars $10.00

D WHAT'S THE AMOUNT?

1. _$11.00_   2. _____

3. _____   4. _____

E LISTENING

Listen and circle the amount you hear.

1. ($35.00) $.35   4. $16.00 $61.00

2. $.05 $5.00   5. $7.10 $71.00

3. $.44 $44.00   6. $14.41 $41.14

A WHAT'S MISSING?

1. Ja _n_ u a r y

2. F _ b r u a r y

3. M a _ c h

4. A _ _ i l

5. M _ _

6. J _ _ e

7. J _ _ y

8. A _ g _ _ t

9. S _ _ t _ _ b e r

10. O _ _ o _ e r

11. N _ _ _ _ _ _ _

12. D _ _ _ _ _ _ _

B WRITE THE MONTH

1. January ___February___ March

2. March April _____

3. June _____ August

4. August _____ October

5. October November _____

FEBRUARY

SUN	MON	TUE	WED	THU	FRI	SAT
		1	2	3	4	5	6
7	8	9	10	11	12	13
14	15	16	17	18	19	20
21	22	23	24	25	26	27
28						

C WHAT'S MISSING?

1. S _u_ n d a y

2. M o _ d a y

3. T u e _ d _ _

4. W e _ n e s _ _ _

5. T h _ _ _ d a y

6. F _ _ _ _ _

7. S _ _ _ _ _ _ _

D WRITE THE DAY

1. SUN _____Sunday_____
2. MON _____
3. TUE _____
4. WED _____
5. THU _____
6. FRI _____
7. SAT _____

E MATCHING

1. 6/14/08   March 6, 2000
2. 4/6/90   January 2, 2009
3. 1/2/09   February 1, 2009
4. 2/1/09   June 14, 2008
5. 3/6/00   April 6, 1990

F WRITING

1. What day is it?   It's _____.
2. What year is it?   It's _____.
3. What month is it?   It's _____.
4. What's today's date?   Today is _____.

G LISTENING

Listen and circle the correct answer.

1. (Monday)   Sunday
2. Thursday   Tuesday
3. June   July
4. November   December
5. April 4   April 14
6. May 7   March 7

31

A WHAT'S THE WORD?

SUN	MON	TUE	WED	THU	FRI	SAT
		1	2	3	4	5	6
7	8	9	10	11	12	13

SUN	MON	TUE	WED	THU	FRI	SAT
		1	2	3	4	5	6
7	8	9	10	11	12	13

Today	Tomorrow	Yesterday

last	next	this

Today is March 2nd.

1. ___Today___ is Tuesday.

2. _____ was Monday.

3. _____ is Wednesday.

Today is March 10th.

4. March 12th is _____ week.

5. March 1st was _____ week.

6. March 16th is _____ week.

B WRITING

Write these dates in numbers.

1. What's today's date?   _ _ / _ _ / _ _

2. What's tomorrow's date?   _ _ / _ _ / _ _

3. What was yesterday's date? _ _ / _ _ / _ _

4/3/11

APR
3
2011

C WHAT'S THE SEASON?

_ _ _ _ _ _   _ _ _ _ _ _   _ _ _ _   _ _ _ _ _ _

A CHOOSE THE CORRECT ANSWER

1. a. She lives in a house.
    (b.) She lives in an apartment.

2. a. He lives in a dormitory.
    b. He lives on a ranch.

3. a. They live on a houseboat.
    b. They live in a mobile home.

4. a. We live on a farm.
    b. We live in the city.

B WHAT TYPE OF HOUSING?

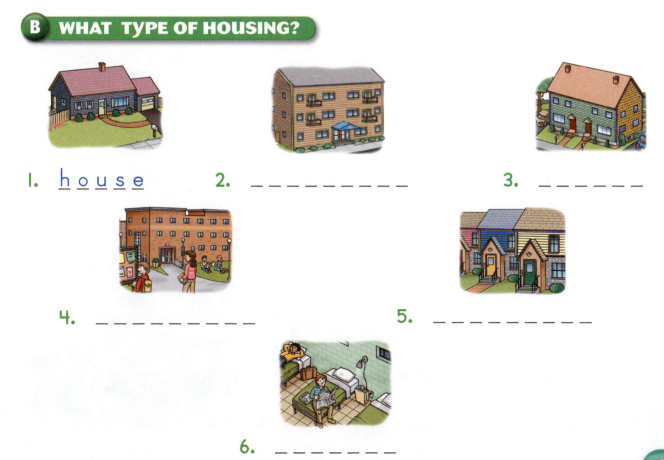

1. h o u s e

2. _ _ _ _ _ _ _ _ _ _

3. _ _ _ _ _ _

4. _ _ _ _ _ _ _ _ _ _

5. _ _ _ _ _ _ _ _ _ _

6. _ _ _ _ _ _ _

33

A CIRCLE THE CORRECT WORD

1. mantel
(bookcase)

2. sofa
armchair

3. rug
picture

4. floor
ceiling

5. painting
window

6. television
DVD player

B WHERE IS IT?

Look at page 21 of the dictionary. Write the correct word.

1. There's a l a m p on the end table.

2. There's a p _ _ _ _ _ on the sofa.

3. There are d _ _ _ _ _ on the window.

4. There's a p _ _ _ _ behind the sofa.

5. There's a p _ _ _ _ _ _ _ above the fireplace.

C WHAT'S THE WORD?

bookcase	lamp	plant	sofa	window
fireplace	pillow	rug	television	

1. _____rug_____

2. _____

3. _____

4. _____

5. _____

6. _____

7. _____

8. _____

9. _____

D JOURNAL

In my living room there is _____

_____.

35

A WHAT'S IN THE DINING ROOM?

1. t a b l e

2. c _ _ _ _ _

3. c _ _ _ _ _ _

4. t _ _ _ _ _

5. p _ _ _ _ _ _ _

6. p _ _ _ _

B MATCHING

1. china   bowl

2. salt   dish

3. butter   shaker

4. salad   pot

5. coffee   cabinet

C LISTENING

Listen and circle the words you hear.

1. (butter dish)   salt shaker   4. table   tablecloth

2. teapot   pitcher   5. teapot   coffee pot

3. salt shaker   pepper shaker   6. creamer   sugar bowl

WHAT IS IT?

bowl	fork	glass	mug	spoon	vase

1. _____spoon_____

2. _____

3. _____

4. _____

5. _____

6. _____

E **WHERE IS IT?**

Look at page 22 of the dictionary. Write the correct word.

1. The platter is on the t a b l e.

2. The fork is on the n _ _ _ _ _.

3. The knife is to the left of the s _ _ _ _.

4. The cup is on the s _ _ _ _ _.

5. The g _ _ _ _ is to the right of the mug.

6. The p _ _ _ _ is between the fork and the knife.

7. The pitcher is on the b _ _ _ _ _.

8. The c _ _ _ _ _ _ _ _ _ is above the table.

A WHAT'S THE WORD?

| bed | blanket | blinds | dresser | mirror | pillow |

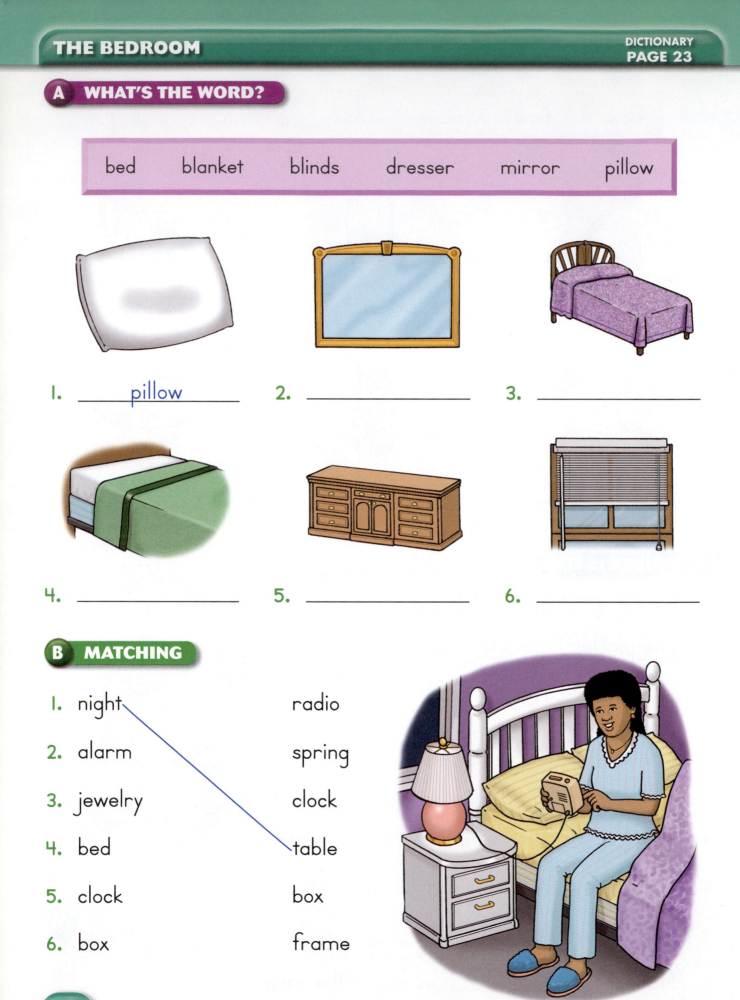

1. _____pillow_____

2. _____

3. _____

4. _____

5. _____

6. _____

B MATCHING

1. night   radio

2. alarm   spring

3. jewelry   clock

4. bed   table

5. clock   box

6. box   frame

WHERE IS IT?

Look at page 23 of the dictionary. Write the correct word.

1. The pillow is on the <u>b e d</u>.

2. The jewelry box is on the _ _ _ _ _ _ _.

3. The box spring is below the _ _ _ _ _ _ _ _.

4. The alarm clock is on the _ _ _ _ _ _ _ _ _ _.

5. The _ _ _ _ _ _ _ is over the dresser.

6. The _ _ _ _ _ _ _ _ _ are on the window.

 **LISTENING**

Listen and circle the words you hear.

1. (blanket)
    blinds

2. mattress
    dresser

3. bedspread
    box spring

4. dresser
    mirror

5. pillow
    blanket

6. alarm clock
    clock radio

E **JOURNAL**

In my bedroom there is _____

_____

_____.

A WHAT'S IN THE KITCHEN?

| blender | dishwasher | oven | sink | toaster |
| cabinet | microwave | oven refrigerator | stove | |

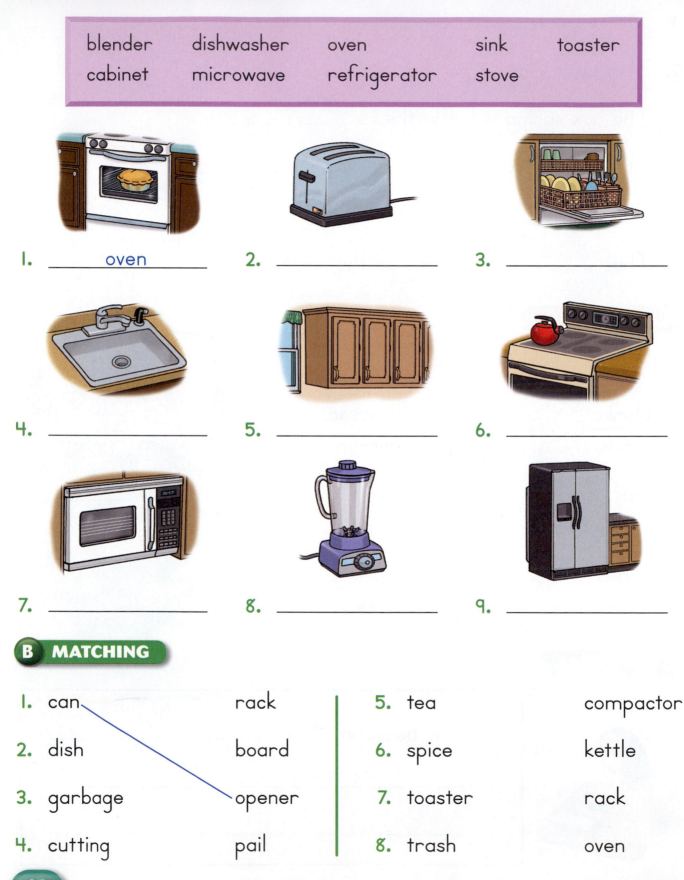

1. _____oven_____

2. _____

3. _____

4. _____

5. _____

6. _____

7. _____

8. _____

9. _____

B MATCHING

1. can   rack

2. dish   board

3. garbage   opener

4. cutting   pail

5. tea   compactor

6. spice   kettle

7. toaster   rack

8. trash   oven

A WHAT IS IT?

car seat	crib	doll	high chair	stroller	swing

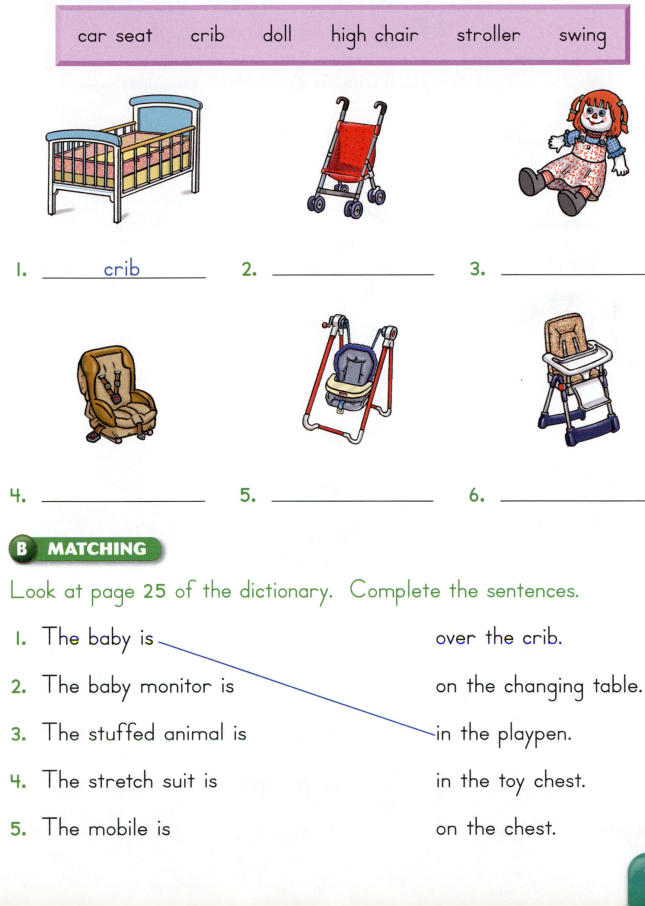

1. _____crib_____

2. _____

3. _____

4. _____

5. _____

6. _____

B MATCHING

Look at page 25 of the dictionary. Complete the sentences.

1. The baby is   over the crib.

2. The baby monitor is   on the changing table.

3. The stuffed animal is   in the playpen.

4. The stretch suit is   in the toy chest.

5. The mobile is   on the chest.

41

A WHAT'S IN THE BATHROOM?

bath mat	mirror	shower	soap	toothbrush
bathtub	plunger	sink	toilet	

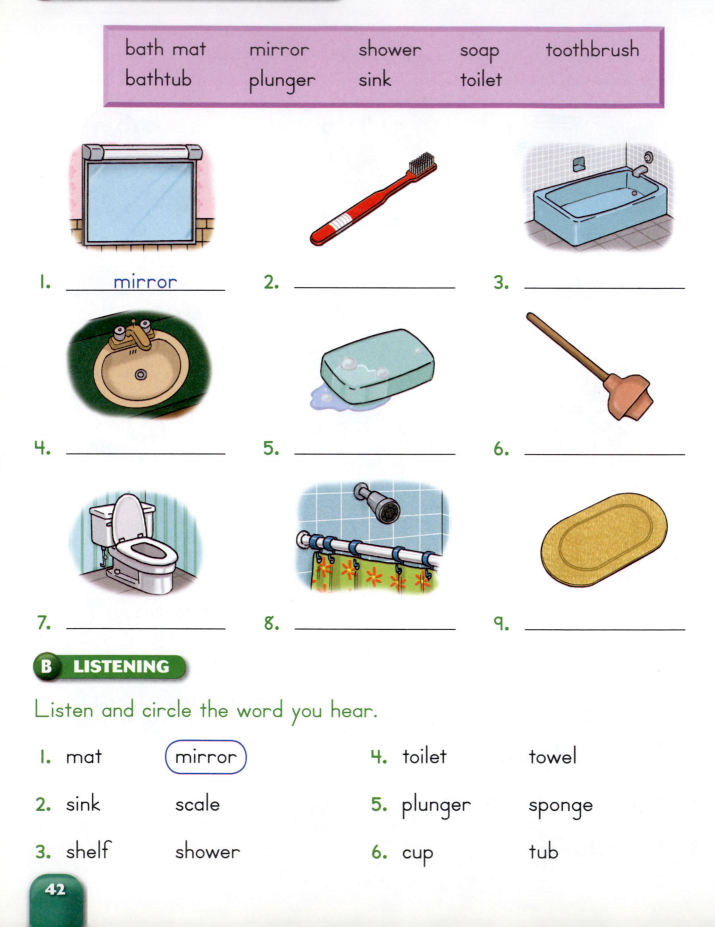

1. ___mirror___   2. _____   3. _____

4. _____   5. _____   6. _____

7. _____   8. _____   9. _____

B LISTENING

Listen and circle the word you hear.

1. mat   (mirror)   4. toilet   towel

2. sink   scale   5. plunger   sponge

3. shelf   shower   6. cup   tub

A WHAT IS IT?

chimney   garage   lamppost   lawnmower   mailbox   window

1. _window_

2. _____

3. _____

4. _____

5. _____

6. _____

B MATCHING

1. door knob   garage

2. letter   lawnmower

3. television   door

4. grass   mailbox

5. car   satellite dish

43

A CHOOSE THE CORRECT WORD

1. classified ad
   (vacancy sign)

2. lease
   tenant

3. lock
   key

4. fire escape
   balcony

5. whirlpool
   air conditioner

6. trash bin
   moving truck

B MATCHING

1. moving   conditioner

2. parking   pool

3. building   garage

4. swimming      truck

5. air   deposit

6. security   manager

1. <u>m a i l b o x</u>

2. _ _ _ _ _ _ _ _ _

3. _ _ _ _ _ _ _ _ _

4. _ _ _ _ _ _ _ _ _

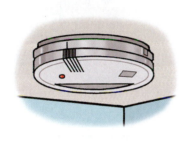

5. _ _ _ _ _

6. _ _ _ _ _ _ _ _

   _ _ _ _ _ _ _ _

   _ _ _ _

D **MATCHING**

1. smoke   lock

2. fire   detector

3. garbage   system

4. dead-bolt   exit

5. sprinkler   room

6. laundry   chute

A WHO IS IT?

| carpenter | electrician | locksmith | painter | plumber | roofer |

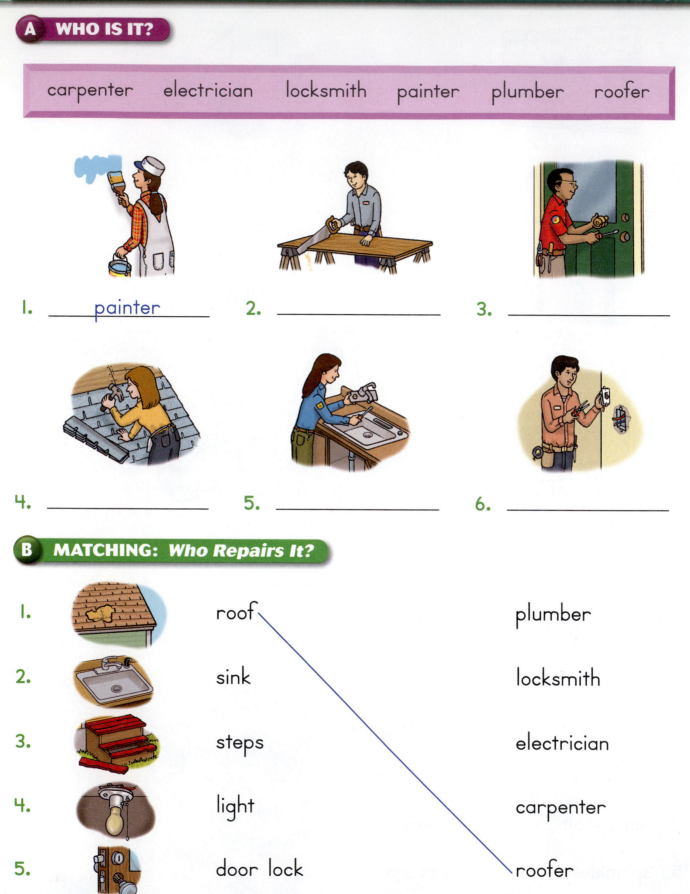

1. painter

2. _____

3. _____

4. _____

5. _____

6. _____

B MATCHING: *Who Repairs It?*

1. roof   plumber

2. sink   locksmith

3. steps   electrician

4. light   carpenter

5. door lock   roofer

WHAT ARE THEY?

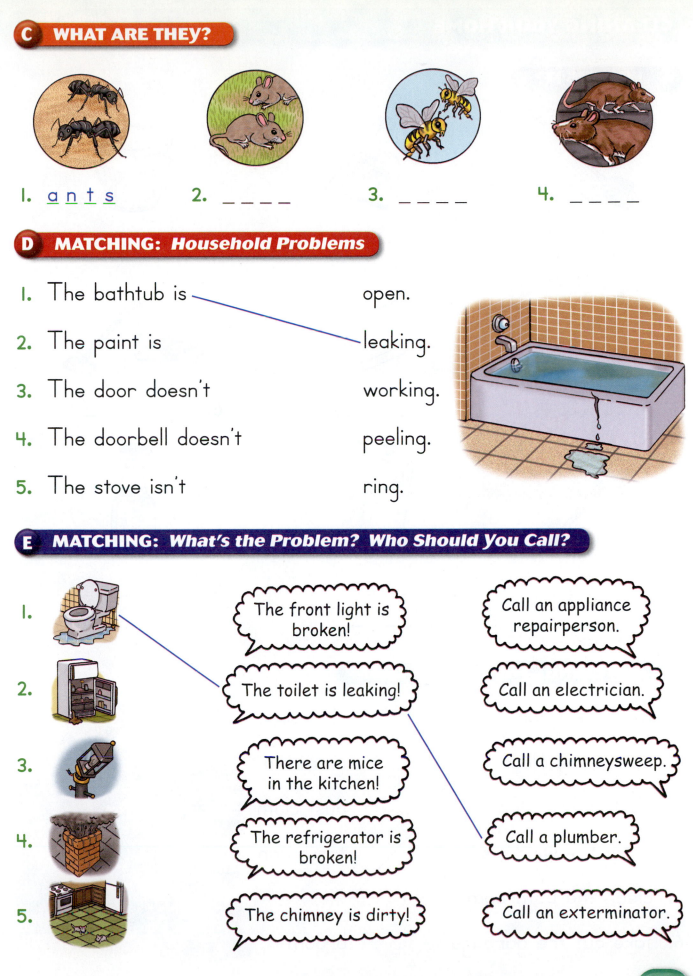

1. a n t s   2. _ _ _ _   3. _ _ _ _   4. _ _ _ _

D MATCHING: Household Problems

1. The bathtub is   open.
2. The paint is   leaking.
3. The door doesn't   working.
4. The doorbell doesn't   peeling.
5. The stove isn't   ring.

E MATCHING: What's the Problem? Who Should You Call?

1.
2.
3.
4.
5.

The front light is broken!

The toilet is leaking!

There are mice in the kitchen!

The refrigerator is broken!

The chimney is dirty!

Call an appliance repairperson.

Call an electrician.

Call a chimneysweep.

Call a plumber.

Call an exterminator.

47

A WHAT IS IT?

1. <u>m o p</u>

2. _ _ _ _ _ _ _ _

3. _ _ _ _ _ _

4. _ _ _ _ _ _

5. _ _ _ _ _ _ _

6. _ _ _ _ _ _

7. _ _ _ _ _ _
   _ _ _ _ _

8. _ _ _ _ _ _
   _ _ _ _ _

9. _ _ _ _ _ _
   _ _ _ _ _ _

B MATCHING: *What Do You Use?*

1. mop the floor   cleanser
2. sweep the floor   ammonia
3. dust   dust cloth
4. wash the windows   trash can
5. clean the bathroom   mop
6. take out the garbage   broom

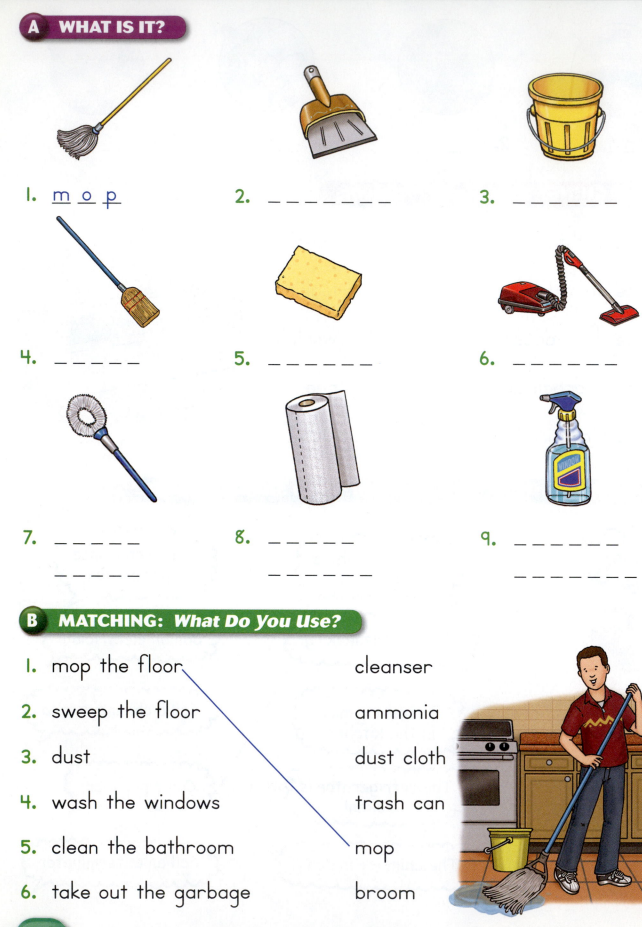

A WHAT IS IT?

1. <u>p a i n t</u>

2. _ _ _ _ _ _ _ _

3. _ _ _ _ _ _ _ _ _ _ _

4. _ _ _ _ _

5. _ _ _ _ _ _ _ _ _

6. _ _ _ _ _ _ _ _ _

7. _ _ _
_ _ _ _ _

8. _ _ _
_ _ _ _ _ _

9. _ _ _ _
_ _ _ _ _ _

B WHERE ARE THEY?

Look at page 33 of the dictionary. Write the correct word.

1. The <u>y a r d s t i c k</u> is to the left of the fly swatter.

2. The _ _ _ _ is to the right of the oil.

3. The _ _ _ _ _ _ _ _ _ are next to the lightbulbs.

4. The _ _ _ _ _ _ _ _ _ is under the step ladder.

5. The paint roller is in the _ _ _ _ _ _ _ _.

6. The _ _ _ _ _ _ _ _ _ _ _ is between the plunger and the tape measure.

49

A WHAT IS IT?

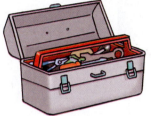

1. <u>s a w</u>

2. _ _ _ _ _ _

3. _ _

4. _ _ _ _ _ _

5. _ _ _ _ _ _ _

6. _ _ _ _ _ _

7. _ _ _ _

8. _ _ _ _ _

9. _ _ _ _ _ _ _ _ _ _ _

B MATCHING

1. circular   wrench

2. Phillips   stripper

3. monkey   drill

4. hand   screwdriver

5. wire   saw

A WHAT IS IT?

1. <u>r a k e</u>

2. _ _ _ _ _

3. _ _ _ _ _ _ _ _

4. _ _ _ _ _ _ _

5. _ _ _

6. _ _ _ _ _ _ _ _ _ _

7. _ _ _ _ _ _ _

8. _ _ _ _ _ _ _

9. _ _ _ _ _ _ _ _ _

B WHAT DO YOU USE?

1. rake leaves   garden hose

2. mow the lawn   pruning shears

3. water the flowers   lawnmower

4. plant vegetables   rake

5. trim the hedge   seeds

6. prune the bushes   clippers

51

A WHAT'S THE PLACE?

bank	cleaners	drug store	gas station
bakery	book store	grocery store	coffee shop
clinic	card store	bus station	day-care center

1. ___bakery___

2. _____

3. _____

4. _____

5. _____

6. _____

7. _____

8. _____

9. _____

10. _____

11. _____

12. _____

52

B MATCHING

1. flower shop   pharmacy

2. gas station   day-care center

3. drug store   service station

4. eye-care center   florist

5. child-care center   optician

C MATCHING

1.    television   bank

2.   money   gas station

3.   hair   electronics store

4.   food   barber shop

5. 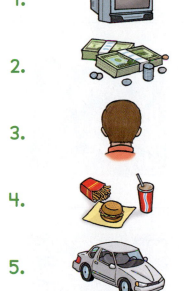   car   fast-food restaurant

D LISTENING

Listen and circle the place you hear.

1. barber shop
   (coffee shop)

2. book store
   drug store

3. clothing store
   furniture store

4. computer store
   convenience store

5. copy center
   eye-care center

6. bus station
   gas station

53

A WHAT'S THE PLACE?

mall	school	restaurant	toy store
park	library	laundromat	health club
hotel	hospital	supermarket	post office

1. _____park_____

2. _____

3. _____

4. _____

5. _____

6. _____

7. _____

8. _____

9. _____

10. _____

11. _____

12. _____

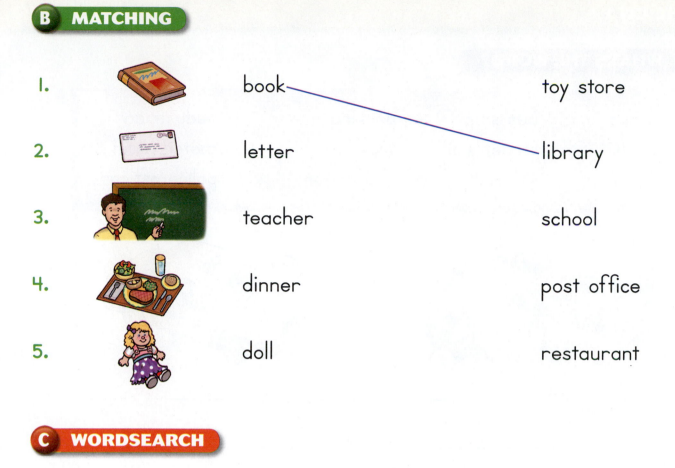

1. book ——— library
2. letter   toy store
3. teacher   school
4. dinner   post office
5. doll   restaurant

C **WORDSEARCH**

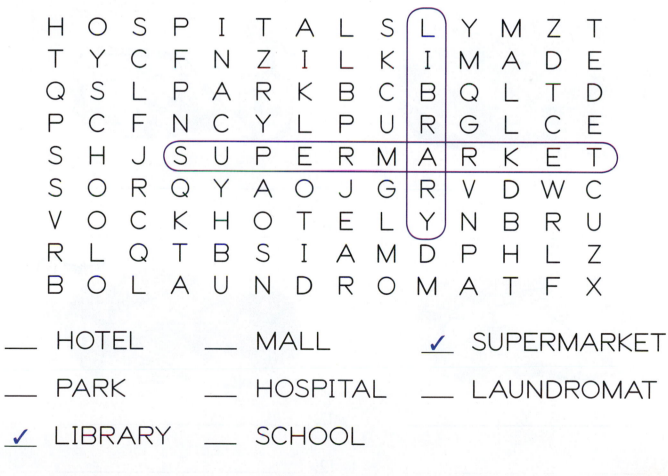

H	O	S	P	I	T	A	L	S	L	Y	M	Z	T
T	Y	C	F	N	Z	I	L	K	I	M	A	D	E
Q	S	L	P	A	R	K	B	C	B	Q	L	T	D
P	C	F	N	C	Y	L	P	U	R	G	L	C	E
S	H	J	S	U	P	E	R	M	A	R	K	E	T
S	O	R	Q	Y	A	O	J	G	R	V	D	W	C
V	O	C	K	H	O	T	E	L	Y	N	B	R	U
R	L	Q	T	B	S	I	A	M	D	P	H	L	Z
B	O	L	A	U	N	D	R	O	M	A	T	F	X

___ HOTEL ___ MALL ✔ SUPERMARKET

___ PARK ___ HOSPITAL ___ LAUNDROMAT

✔ LIBRARY ___ SCHOOL

A WHAT'S THE WORD?

bus	bus stop	parking meter	pedestrian
taxi	street sign	traffic light	meter maid
sewer	sidewalk	taxi driver	police officer

1. _____bus_____

3. _____

2. _____

4. _____

5. _____

7. _____

6. _____

8. _____

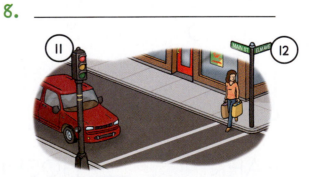

9. _____

11. _____

10. _____

12. _____

MATCHING

1. police   light
2. parking   container
3. trash   station
4. traffic   hydrant
5. fire   meter

C **WHICH GROUP?**

| bus driver | intersection | police officer | taxi driver |
| bus stop | pedestrian | police station | taxi stand |

People   Places

bus driver
_____   _____

_____   _____

_____   _____

_____   _____

D **YES OR NO?**

Look at pages 40–41 of the dictionary. Answer Yes or No.

No   1. The police officer is on the sidewalk.

_____   2. The police officer is in the intersection.

_____   3. The fire station is next to the courthouse.

_____   4. The city hall is next to the courthouse.

_____   5. The garbage truck is at the bus stop.

A WHAT'S THE WORD?

baby	boy	girl	man	senior citizens	woman

a. _____boy_____   c. _____   e. _____

b. _____   d. _____   f. _____

B WHAT'S THE WORD?

middle-aged	old	young

a. _____young_____

b. _____

c. _____

average weight	heavy	slim

d. _____

e. _____

f. _____

58

| heavy | old | short | tall | thin | young |

Height	Weight	Age
	heavy	
_____	_____	_____
_____	_____	_____

D **WHAT DO THEY LOOK LIKE?**

| black | blond | brown | red |

1. 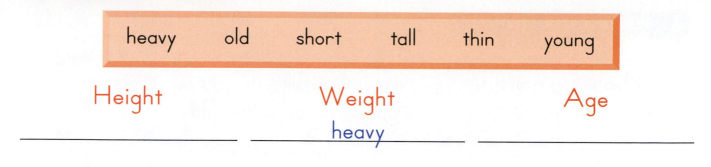 She has long _____blond_____ hair.

2. He has short _____ hair.

3. She has long _____ hair.

4. She has shoulder-length _____ hair.

| bald | curly | mustache | wavy |

5. He has _____ gray hair.

6. She has _____ brown hair.

7. He's _____.

8. He has a _____.

E **JOURNAL:** *What Do You Look Like?*

I have _____.

A   WHAT'S THE WORD?

clean	difficult	easy	full	new	open
closed	dirty	empty	large	old	small

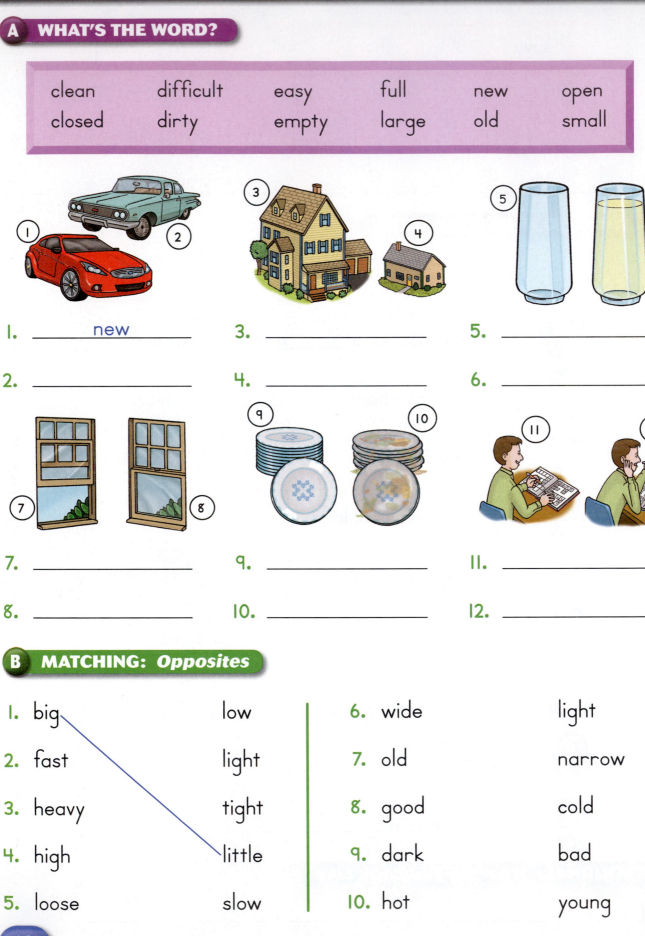

1. _____new_____

2. _____

3. _____

4. _____

5. _____

6. _____

7. _____

8. _____

9. _____

10. _____

11. _____

12. _____

B   MATCHING: *Opposites*

1. big   low
2. fast   light
3. heavy   tight
4. high   little
5. loose   slow

6. wide   light
7. old   narrow
8. good   cold
9. dark   bad
10. hot   young

C WHAT'S THE WORD?

cold	dull	heavy	messy	narrow	plain	single	wet

1. Is the water hot?

   No. It's <u>c o l d</u>.

2. Is she married?

   No. She's _ _ _ _ _ _.

3. Is the street wide?

   No. It's _ _ _ _ _ _.

4. Is the dress fancy?

   No. It's _ _ _ _ _.

5. Is the box light?

   No. It's _ _ _ _ _.

6. Is the knife sharp?

   No. It's _ _ _ _.

7. Is his room neat?

   No. It's _ _ _ _ _.

8. Are the clothes dry?

   No. They're _ _ _.

61

A LISTENING

Listen. Put a check under the correct picture.

1. _____ ✔_____

2. _____ _____

3. _____ _____

4. _____ _____

5. _____ _____

6. _____ _____

7. _____ _____

8. _____ _____

9. _____ _____

10. _____ _____

1. shocked
   (proud)

2. happy
   afraid

3. tired
   surprised

4. upset
   exhausted

5. annoyed
   embarrassed

6. jealous
   nervous

C **WHAT'S THE WORD?**

1. <u>s a d</u>

2. _ _ _ _

3. _ _ _ _ _ _ _ _

4. _ _ _ _

5. _ _ _ _ _ _ _ _ _

6. _ _ _ _ _ _ _

D **JOURNAL**

I feel _____ today

because _____

_____ .

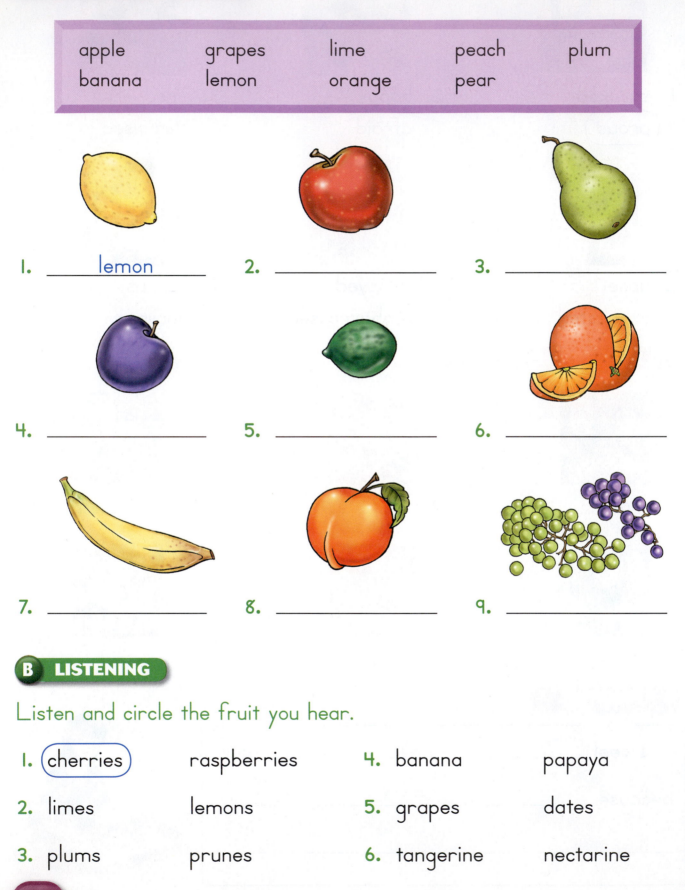

A   WHAT'S THE WORD?

apple	grapes	lime	peach	plum
banana	lemon	orange	pear	

1. _____lemon_____

2. _____

3. _____

4. _____

5. _____

6. _____

7. _____

8. _____

9. _____

B   LISTENING

Listen and circle the fruit you hear.

1. (cherries)   raspberries

2. limes   lemons

3. plums   prunes

4. banana   papaya

5. grapes   dates

6. tangerine   nectarine

A WHAT'S THE WORD?

1. <u>t o m a t o</u>

2. _ _ _ _ _ _

3. _ _ _ _ _ _ _

4. _ _ _ _

5. _ _ _ _ _ _ _

6. _ _ _ _ _ _

7. _ _ _ _ _ _ _ _

8. _ _ _ _ _ _ _ _

9. _ _ _ _ _ _ _ _

B MATCHING

1. acorn   potato

2. red   bean

3. sweet   squash

4. lima   sprout

5. brussels   pepper

A CHOOSE THE CORRECT WORD

1. steak
   (turkey)

2. ground beef
   salmon

3. lamb chops
   sausages

4. clams
   crabs

5. liver
   roast beef

6. shrimp
   lobster

B WHAT'S THE WORD?

1. s a l m o n

2. c _ _ _ _ _ _ _

3. s _ _ _ _

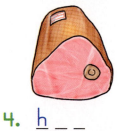

4. h _ _

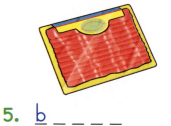

5. b _ _ _ _

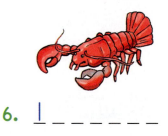

6. l _ _ _ _ _ _

C WHICH GROUP?

| duck | haddock | ribs | sausages | trout | turkey |

Meat	Poultry	Seafood
	duck	

A WHAT'S THE WORD?

1. m i l k

2. _ _ _ _ _ _ _

3. _ _ _ _ _

4. _ _ _ _ _ _ _

5. _ _ _ _ _

6. _ _ _ _ _ _ _ _

7. _ _ _ _ _

8. _ _ _ _ _ _ _

9. _ _ _ _ _ _

10. _ _ _ _ _ _ _ _ _ _

11. _ _ _ _ _ _ _ _ _ _ _ _

B WHICH GROUP?

| apple juice | butter | fruit punch |
| bottled water | diet soda | margarine |

Dairy Products	Juices	Beverages
	apple juice	
_____	_____	_____
_____	_____	_____

67

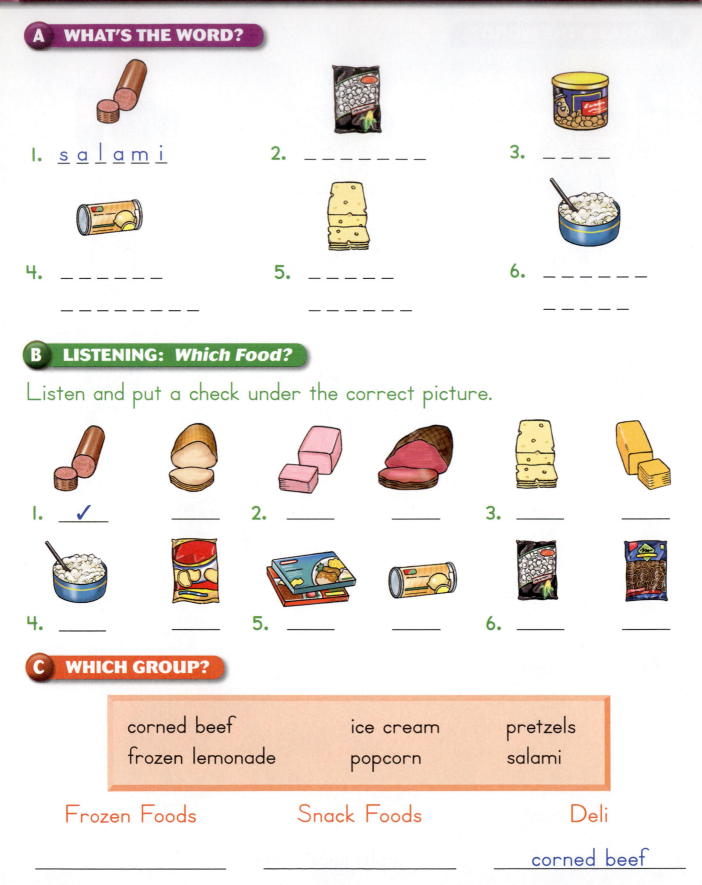

A WHAT'S THE WORD?

1. s a l a m i

2. _ _ _ _ _ _ _ _ _

3. _ _ _ _ _

4. _ _ _ _ _ _ _
   _ _ _ _ _ _ _ _

5. _ _ _ _ _
   _ _ _ _ _

6. _ _ _ _ _ _ _
   _ _ _ _ _

B LISTENING: *Which Food?*

Listen and put a check under the correct picture.

1. ✓ _____

2. _____ _____

3. _____ _____

4. _____ _____

5. _____ _____

6. _____ _____

C WHICH GROUP?

| corned beef | ice cream | pretzels |
| frozen lemonade | popcorn | salami |

Frozen Foods	Snack Foods	Deli
		corned beef
_____	_____	_____
_____	_____	_____

A WHAT'S THE WORD?

bread	cookies	jelly	mayonnaise	salsa	soup
cereal	flour	ketchup	rice	salt	spaghetti

1. ketchup

2. _____

3. _____

4. _____

5. _____

6. _____

7. _____

8. _____

9. _____

10. _____

11. _____

12. _____

B WHICH GROUP?

bread	cereal	mustard	noodles	pickles	rolls

Packaged Goods   Condiments   Baked Goods

                                                    bread

_____   _____   _____

_____   _____   _____

A WHAT'S THE WORD?

1. s o a p

2. _ _ _ _ _ _ _ _

3. _ _ _ _ _ _ _ _

4. _ _ _ _ _ _ _ _

5. _ _ _ _ _

6. _ _ _ _ _ _ _ _

7. _ _ _
   _ _ _ _ _

8. _ _ _ _
   _ _ _ _

9. _ _ _
   _ _ _ _

10. _ _ _ _ _ _
    _ _ _ _ _ _

11. _ _ _ _ _ _
    _ _ _ _

12. _ _ _ _ _ _ _ _
    _ _ _ _

B WHICH GROUP?

| diapers | napkins | soap |
| formula | plastic wrap | tissues |

Paper Products   Baby Products   Household Items

_____   diapers   _____

_____   _____   _____

70

A CHOOSE THE CORRECT WORD

1. customer
   (cashier)

2. aisle
   scale

3. shopper
   packer

4. checkout line
   cash register

5. plastic bag
   paper bag

6. scale
   counter

7. shopping cart
   checkout counter

8. plastic bag
   shopping basket

9. clerk
   scanner

B WHICH GROUP?

bagger	paper bag
cashier	scale
counter	scanner
manager	shopper

People

bagger
_____
_____
_____

Things

_____
_____
_____
_____

A WHAT'S THE WORD?

bag	box	can		dozen	head	loaf	pound
bottle	bunch	container		gallon	jar	pint	quart

1. a _dozen_ eggs

2. a _____ of soup

3. a _____ of flour

4. a _____ of jam

5. a _____ of lettuce

6. a _____ of carrots

7. a _____ of cookies

8. a _____ of butter

9. a _____ of bread

10. a _____ of yogurt

11. a _____ of milk

12. a _____ of ice cream

13. a _____ of milk

14. a _____ of ketchup

1. a jar of
2. a box of
3. a bottle of
4. a bunch of
5. a can of
6. a dozen
7. a roll of
8. a head of

soda
cabbage
eggs
tuna fish
cereal
baby food
paper towels
bananas

C WORDSEARCH

```
L  S  A  P  Q  M  W  R  V  G  Q  N  B  S
S  C  B  E  O  Y  J  L  O  A  F  B  D  D
O  A  R  S  B  Q  J  A  B  L  O  K  O  C
A  N  E  F  P  I  N  T  V  L  D  J  B  B
R  I  H  R  S  Q  D  S  N  O  L  A  D  S
B  R  Q  O  X  Z  N  I  F  N  E  R  V  B
U  B  O  T  T  L  E  B  M  X  P  A  S  T
Q  A  O  L  A  R  J  Z  L  D  O  Z  E  N
A  G  M  P  O  U  N  D  O  N  B  U  E  Y
```

___ BAG   ___ DOZEN   ___ PINT

___ BOTTLE   ___ JAR   ___ POUND

___ CAN   ✓ LOAF   ✓ GALLON

73

A MATCHING

1. Tbsp.   ounce

2. pt.   gallon

3. gal.   tablespoon

4. lb.   fluid ounce

5. oz.   pound

6. tsp.   pint

7. fl. oz.   teaspoon

B WHAT'S THE NUMBER?

1. 1 cup = __8__ fl. ozs.

2. 1 gal. = ___ fl. ozs.

3. 16 fl. ozs. = ___ pt.

4. 1 qt. = ___ fl. ozs.

5. 1 lb. = ___ ozs.

6. 1/2 lb. = ___ ozs.

C LISTENING

Listen and circle the amount you hear.

1. (ounce)   gallon   4. 8 lbs.   8 ozs.

2. Tbsp.   tsp.   5. 1/4 lb.   3/4 lb.

3. lb.   oz.   6. cup   quart

A   CHOOSE THE CORRECT WORD

1. stir
   (slice)

2. bake
   boil

3. mix
   grate

4. fry
   steam

5. peel
   pour

6. beat
   cut

B   MATCHING

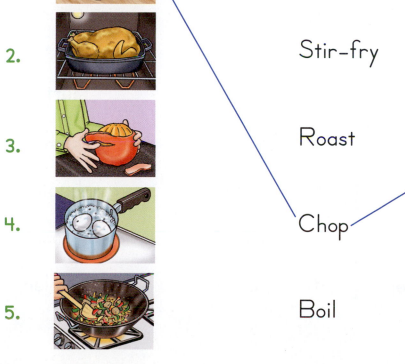

1.

2.

3.

4.

5.

Peel   the turkey.

Stir-fry   the eggs.

Roast   the onions.

Chop   the vegetables.

Boil   the orange.

A WHAT IS IT?

1. g r a t e r

2. _ _ _

3. _ _ _

4. _ _ _ _ _

5. _ _ _ _ _ _ _ _ _

6. _ _ _ _ _ _

7. _ _ _ _ _ _ _ _

8. _ _ _ _ _ _ _

9. _ _ _ _ _ _ _

B MATCHING

1. pie   bowl
2. mixing   pin
3. rolling   plate
4. can   pan
5. roasting   opener

6. vegetable   cutter
7. egg   knife
8. carving   beater
9. cookie   scoop
10. ice cream   peeler

A WHAT'S THE WORD?

1. t a c o

2. _ _ _ _ _

3. _ _ _ _ _

4. _ _ _ _

5. _ _ _ _ _ _

6. _ _ _ _ _ _ _ _ _

7. _ _ _ _ _ _ _ _ _ _

8. _ _ _   _ _ _

9. _ _ _   _ _ _ _ _

B WHICH GROUP?

burrito   lid   milkshake   napkin   salad   straw   taco   utensil

Restaurant Supplies		Fast Food	
_____	_____	burrito	_____
_____	_____	_____	_____

C LISTENING

Listen. Write the number under the correct picture.

___   ___   1   ___   ___   ___

A WHAT'S THE WORD?

1. <u>d o n u t</u>

2. _ _ _ _ _ _

3. _ _ _ _ _ _ _

4. _ _ _

5. _ _ _ _ _ _ _

6. _ _ _ _ _ _ _ _

7. _ _ _ _ _ _ _

8. _ _ _ _ _ _ _ _

9. _ _ _ _ _

B WHICH GROUP?

biscuit   coffee   donut   lemonade   milk   pastry   sandwich   tea

eat   drink

_____biscuit_____   _____ | _____   _____

_____   _____ | _____   _____

C LISTENING

Listen. Write the number under the correct picture.

___   ___   1   ___   ___   ___

A WHAT'S THE WORD?

booth	chef	high chair	table	waitress
check	dishwasher	menu	waiter	

1. _____booth_____

2. _____

3. _____

4. _____

5. _____

6. _____

7. _____

8. _____

9. _____

B LISTENING

Listen. Write the number under the correct picture.

____   ____   ____   1   ____   ____

A CHOOSE THE CORRECT WORD

1. pie
   (cake)

2. nachos
   noodles

3. jello
   ice cream

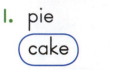

4. french fries
   potato skins

5. salad
   pudding

6. baked potato
   mashed potatoes

B WHAT'S ON THE MENU?

Fill in these words to complete the menu.

rice	pudding	antipasto	broiled fish	mashed potatoes
jello	meatloaf	spaghetti	baked chicken	spinach salad
nachos	fruit cup	roast beef		

Today's Specials

APPETIZERS:
_____fruit cup_____
_____

SALADS:
_____
_____

ENTREES:
_____
_____
_____
_____

SIDE DISHES:
_____
_____

DESSERTS:
_____
_____

A WHAT'S THE COLOR?

1. r e d

2. _ _ _ _ _

3. _ _ _ _ _

4. _ _ _ _ _ _

5. _ _ _ _ _

6. _ _ _ _ _

7. _ _ _ _ _

8. _ _ _ _ _ _

9. _ _ _ _ _ _

B CROSSWORD

ACROSS

2. 　　　　4.

DOWN

1. 　　　　2. 　　　　3.

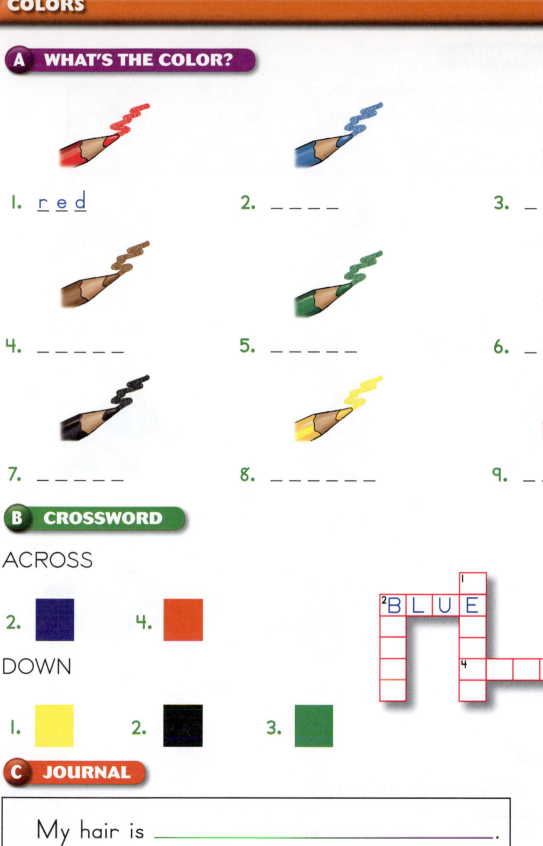

C JOURNAL

My hair is _____.

My eyes are _____.

My favorite color is _____.

A WHAT'S THE WORD?

| blouse | jacket | shirt | skirt | sweater |
| dress | pants | shorts | suit | |

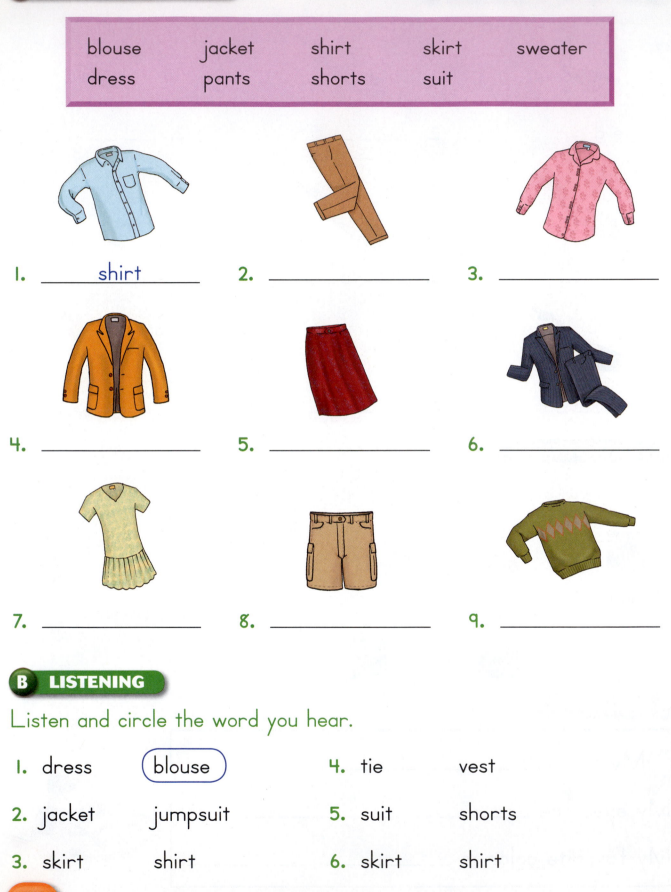

1. _____shirt_____

2. _____

3. _____

4. _____

5. _____

6. _____

7. _____

8. _____

9. _____

B LISTENING

Listen and circle the word you hear.

1. dress   (blouse)   4. tie   vest

2. jacket   jumpsuit   5. suit   shorts

3. skirt   shirt   6. skirt   shirt

A WHAT'S THE WORD?

| cap | gloves | jacket | poncho | sunglasses |
| coat | hat | mittens | raincoat | |

1. _____cap_____

2. _____

3. _____

4. _____

5. _____

6. _____

7. _____

8. _____

9. _____

B WHICH GROUP?

| gloves | overcoat | poncho | raincoat | ski hat | umbrella |

It's raining!   It's cold!

_____   ____gloves____

_____   _____

_____   _____

A WHAT'S THE WORD?

1. s t o c k i n g s

2. _ _ _ _ _ _ _ _

3. _ _ _ _ _

4. _ _ _ _ _ _ _ _

5. _ _ _ _ _ _ _ _

6. _ _ _ _ _ _ _ _

7. _ _ _ _
   _ _ _ _ _

8. _ _ _ _ _
   _ _ _ _ _

9. _ _ _ _
   _ _ _ _ _ _ _

B WHICH GROUP?

| briefs | nightgown | nightshirt | pajamas | slip | stockings |

Sleepwear	Underwear
	briefs
_____	_____
_____	_____

A **WHAT'S THE WORD?**

boots	sandals	sneakers	sweatshirt	T-shirt
flip-flops	shoes	sweatpants	swimsuit	

1. _swimsuit_

2. _____

3. _____

4. _____

5. _____

6. _____

7. _____

8. _____

9. _____

B **WHICH GROUP?**

boots	leotard	sandals	shoes	swimsuit	T-shirt

Exercise Clothing

Footwear

_____   _boots_

_____   _____

_____   _____

A **CHOOSE THE CORRECT WORD**

1. belt
   (necklace)

2. earrings
   cuff links

3. ring
   key ring

4. wallet
   watch

5. backpack
   makeup bag

6. briefcase
   change purse

B **MATCHING**

1. wedding   watch

2. wrist   bag

3. change   ring

4. book   necklace

5. cuff   links

6. pearl   purse

A CHOOSE THE CORRECT WORD

1. (short-sleeved)
   long-sleeved

2. knee-high socks
   ankle socks

3. V-neck sweater
   turtleneck

4. cardigan sweater
   crewneck sweater

5. striped
   checked

6. plaid
   polka-dotted

B LISTENING

Listen. Put a check under the correct picture.

1. _____   _____ ✔   2. _____   _____

3. _____   _____   4. _____   _____

5. _____   _____   6. _____   _____

A WHAT'S THE WORD?

| heavy | large | long | low | short | tight |
| high | light | loose | narrow | small | wide |

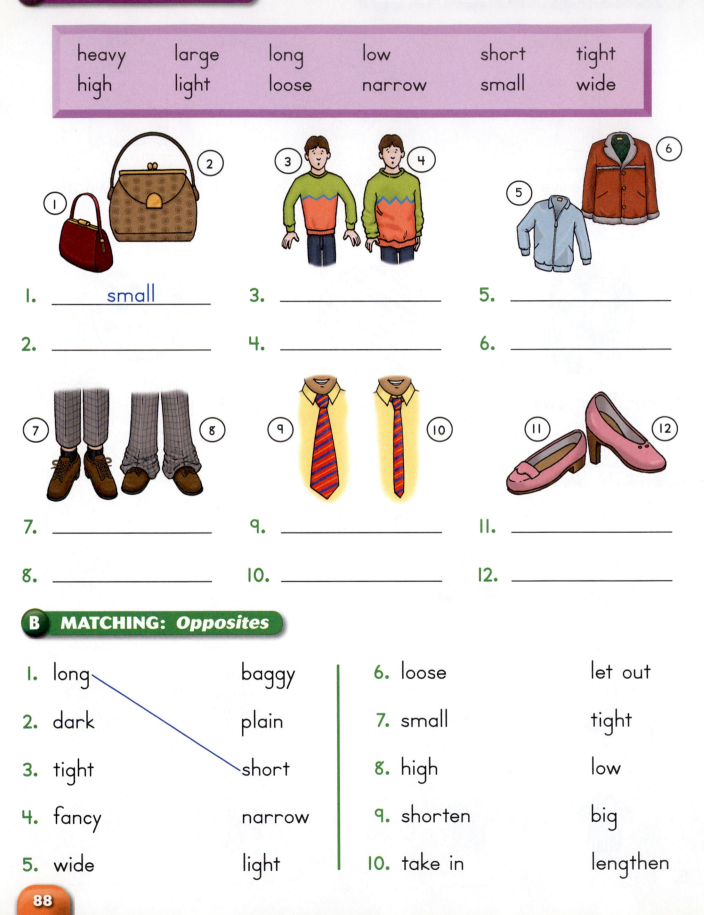

1. _____small_____

2. _____

3. _____

4. _____

5. _____

6. _____

7. _____

8. _____

9. _____

10. _____

11. _____

12. _____

B MATCHING: *Opposites*

1. long   baggy

2. dark   plain

3. tight   short

4. fancy   narrow

5. wide   light

6. loose   let out

7. small   tight

8. high   low

9. shorten   big

10. take in   lengthen

A WHAT'S THE WORD?

1. i r o n

2. _ _ _ _ _ _

3. _ _ _ _ _ _

4. _ _ _ _ _ _

5. _ _ _ _ _ _

6. _ _ _ _ _ _ _ _ _

7. _ _ _ _ _ _ _

8. _ _ _ _ _ _

9. _ _ _ _ _ _ _ _ _ _

B MATCHING

1. spray   detergent

2. laundry   softener

3. ironing   remover

4. fabric   board

5. static cling   trap

6. lint   starch

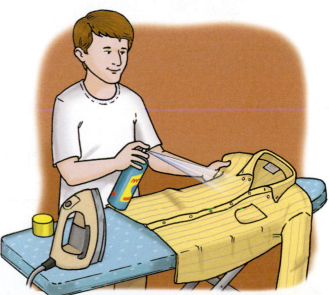

A WHICH DEPARTMENT?

1. sofa — Furniture

Men's Clothing

2. ring

Women's Clothing

3. tie

Housewares

4. stove

Furniture

5. iron

Electronics

6. dress

Household Appliances

7. TV

Jewelry

B MATCHING

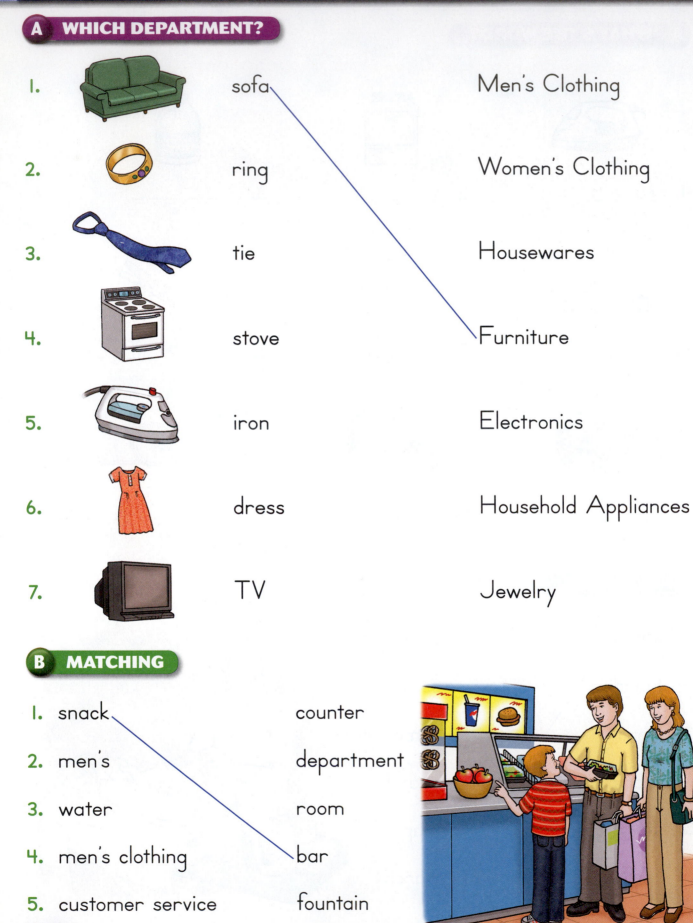

1. snack   counter

2. men's   department

3. water   room

4. men's clothing   bar

5. customer service fountain

A LABEL INFORMATION

Read the sale sign, label, and price tag. Answer the questions.

1. What's the material?   ____100%__ cotton____

2. What's the size?   _____

3. What's the regular price?   _____

4. What's the discount?   _____

5. What's the sale price?   _____

6. What are the care instructions?   _____

B MATCHING: A Store Receipt

Look at the receipt.
Match the information.

Shopper's Mart

Blouse	$30.00
40% off	−12.00
Price	18.00
Tax	.90
Cash	$18.90

1. sale price $18.90

2. discount $30.00

3. regular price $.90

4. total price $18.00

5. sales tax   40% off

A   WHAT'S THE WORD?

a. <u>TV</u>

b. _ _ _ _ _ _ _ _ _

c. _ _ _ _ _

d. _ _ _ _ _ _ _ _ _ _

e. _ _ _ _ _ _ _ _ _ _ _ _

f. _ _ _ _ _ _ _

g. _ _ _ _ _ _ _ _ _

h. _ _ _ _ _ _ _ _ _ _

B   MATCHING

1. clock   control

2. tape   player

3. video game   radio

4. DVD   system

5. remote   recorder

A WHAT'S THE WORD?

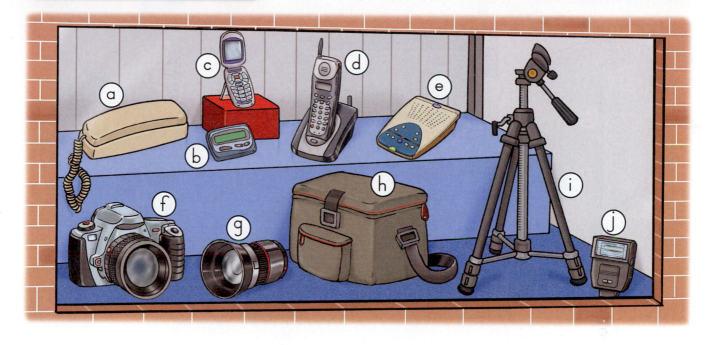

a. <u>t e l e p h o n e</u>

b. _ _ _ _ _

c. _ _ _ _   _ _ _ _ _

d. _ _ _ _ _ _ _ _   _ _ _ _

e. _ _ _ _ _ _ _ _
   _ _ _ _ _ _

f. _ _ _ _ _ _

g. _ _ _ _   _ _ _ _

h. _ _ _ _ _ _   _ _ _ _

i. _ _ _ _ _ _

j. _ _ _ _ _
   _ _ _ _ _ _ _ _ _

B MATCHING

1. digital   phone

2. cell   lens

3. answering   camera

4. zoom   charger

5. battery   machine

A WHAT'S THE WORD?

a. <u>c o m p u t e r</u>

b. _ _ - _ _ _

c. _ _ _ _ _ _ _

d. _ _ _ _ _

e. _ _ _ _ _ _ _ _

f. _ _ _ _ _

g. _ _ _ _ _ _ _ _   _ _ _ _

h. _ _ _ _ _ _ _

B MATCHING

1. notebook   drive

2. disk   screen

3. surge   computer

4. LCD   program

5. software   protector

A WHAT'S THE WORD?

a. <u>b l o c k s</u>

b. _ _ _   _ _ _ _ _

c. _ _ _ _

d. _ _ _ _   _ _ _ _ _

e. _ _ _ _ _ _

f. _ _ _ _ _ _ _   _ _ _ _

g. _ _ _ _ _

h. _ _ _ _ _   _ _ _

i. _ _ _ _ _ _ _

j. _ _ _ _   _ _ _

k. _ _ _ _ _ _ _

l. _ _ _ _ _ _ _ _ _ _

A   CHOOSE THE CORRECT WORD

1. bankbook
   (check)

2. credit card
   currency

3. ATM card
   deposit slip

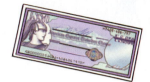

4. traveler's check
   withdrawal slip

5. teller
   account

6. bank officer
   security guard

B   AT THE BANK

Your account number is 4159 8673. Make withdrawals and deposits.

WITHDRAWAL APPLICATION	Date_____	
4159 8673 **Account number**	CASH WITHDRAWAL	$75.00
	CHECK WITHDRAWAL	
	TOTAL WITHDRAWAL	$75.00
_____ Signature		

WITHDRAWAL APPLICATION	Date_____	
4159 8673 **Account number**	CASH WITHDRAWAL	$200.00
	CHECK WITHDRAWAL	
	TOTAL WITHDRAWAL	$200.00
_____ Signature		

1. Withdraw $75.00 (cash).

2. Withdraw $200.00 (cash).

DEPOSIT SLIP	Date_____	
_____ Account number	CURRENCY	
	COIN	
_____ Name	CHECKS	
	LESS CASH	
_____ Sign here ONLY if cash received from deposit	TOTAL	

DEPOSIT SLIP	Date_____	
_____ Account number	CURRENCY	
	COIN	
_____ Name	CHECKS	
	LESS CASH	
_____ Sign here ONLY if cash received from deposit	TOTAL	

3. Deposit $100.00 (cash).

4. Deposit $256.00 (a check).

A WHAT'S THE WORD?

1. b i l l

2. _ _ _ _ _ _

3. _ _ _ _ _ _ _ _ _ _

4. _ _ _ _

5. _ _ _ _ _ _ _

6. _ _ _ _ _ _ _ _ _

B USING AN ATM MACHINE

Put the pictures in order. Write the number under each picture.

1. Insert your ATM card.
2. Enter your pin number.
3. Select a transaction.
4. Get cash.
5. Remove your card.
6. Take your receipt.

_____   _____   1   _____   _____   _____

C PAY THE BILL

City Power

$75.80

1256

_____ 20 _____

Pay to the
Order of _____ $ _____

_____ Dollars

First National Bank
1200 West 45th Street
Chicago, IL 60609

For _____ _____

A012345678A 321 1 123456C 0000

A · WHAT'S THE WORD?

stamp	mailbox	postcard	air letter	letter
zip code	package	envelope	money order	

1. ___envelope___

2. _____

3. _____

4. _____

5. _____

6. _____

7. _____

8. _____

9. _____

B · MATCHING

1. letter   address

2. return   order

3. air   carrier

4. money   post

5. parcel   code

6. zip   letter

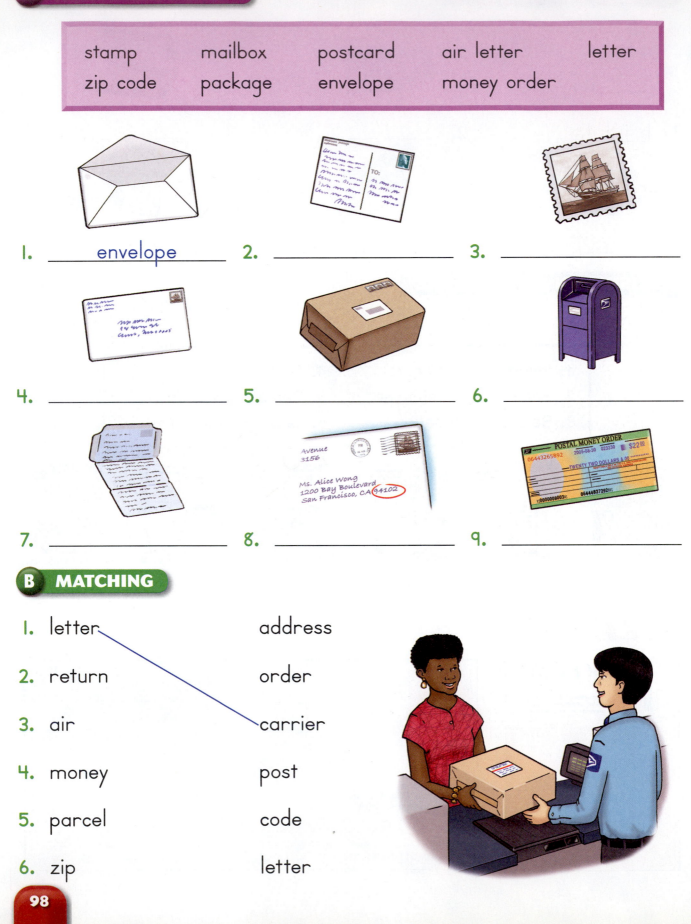

A WHAT'S THE WORD?

| atlas | magazine | librarian | online catalog |
| shelves | newspaper | encyclopedia | checkout desk |

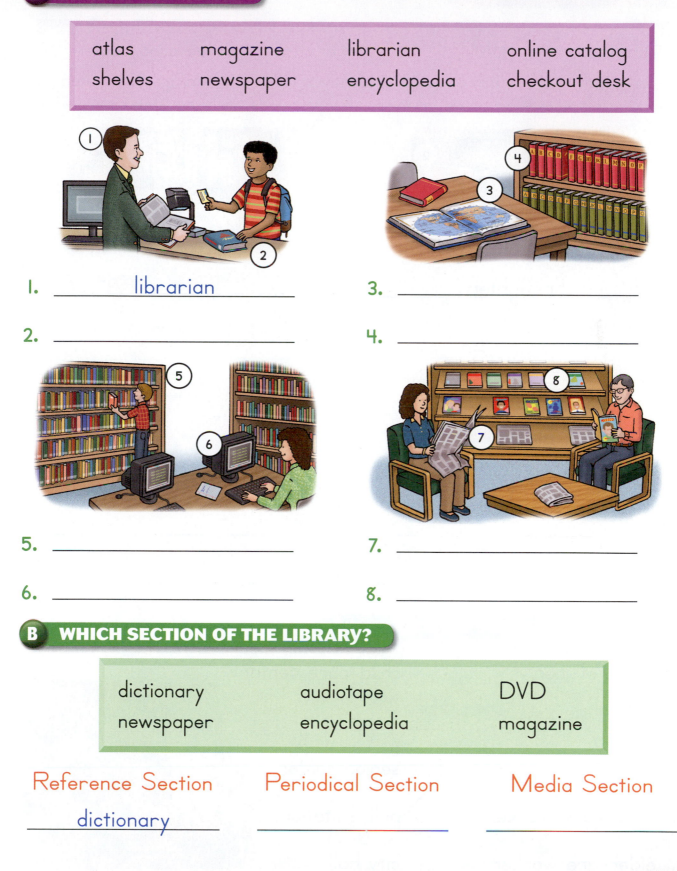

1. ___librarian___

2. _____

3. _____

4. _____

5. _____

6. _____

7. _____

8. _____

B WHICH SECTION OF THE LIBRARY?

| dictionary | audiotape | DVD |
| newspaper | encyclopedia | magazine |

Reference Section	Periodical Section	Media Section
dictionary	_____	_____
_____	_____	_____

A WHAT'S THE WORD?

ambulance	EMT	firefighter	recycling center
city hall	fire engine	mayor	sanitation worker

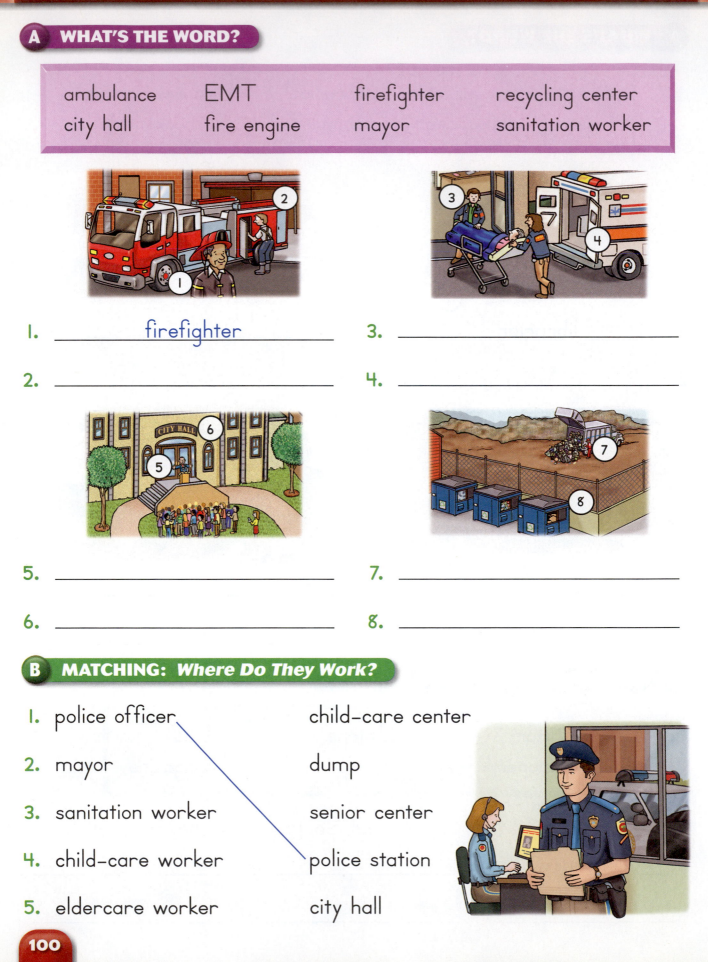

1. _____firefighter_____

2. _____

3. _____

4. _____

5. _____

6. _____

7. _____

8. _____

B MATCHING: *Where Do They Work?*

1. police officer   child-care center

2. mayor   dump

3. sanitation worker   senior center

4. child-care worker   police station

5. eldercare worker   city hall

A WHAT'S THE WORD?

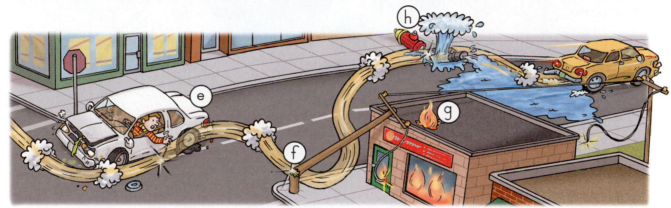

a. <u>b u r g l a r y</u>

b. _ _ _ _ _ _ _

c. _ _ _ _ _ _ _ _ _

d. _ _ _ _ _ _ _

e. _ _ _   _ _ _ _ _ _ _

f. _ _ _ _ _   _ _ _ _   _ _ _ _

g. _ _ _ _

h. _ _ _ _ _   _ _ _ _   _ _ _ _ _

B MATCHING

1. car   spill

2. power   child

3. lost   accident

4. water main   break

5. chemical   outage

101

A **WHAT IS IT?**

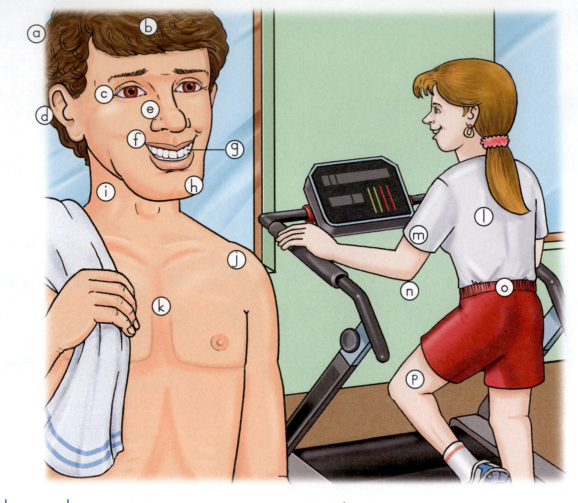

a. <u>h e a d</u>

b. _ _ _ _

c. _ _ _

d. _ _ _

e. _ _ _ _

f. _ _ _ _ _

g. _ _ _ _ _

h. _ _ B O D _

i. _ _ _ _

j. _ _ _ _ _ _ _ _

k. _ _ _ _ _

l. _ _ _ _

m. _ _ _

n. _ _ _ _ _

o. _ _ _ _ _

p. _ _ _

B WHAT IS IT?

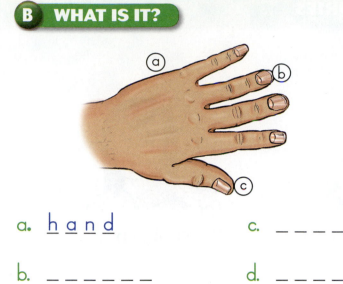
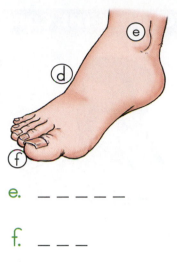

a. <u>h a n d</u>   c. _ _ _ _ _ _   e. _ _ _ _ _ _

b. _ _ _ _ _ _ _   d. _ _ _ _   f. _ _ _

C MATCHING: *Where Are They?*

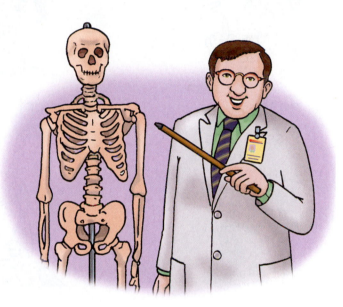

1. throat ——————— foot

2. finger ——————— neck

3. toe   mouth

4. tooth   arm

5. brain   hand

6. elbow   head

D HOW MANY DO WE HAVE?

1. hands   2   6. toes   _____

2. fingers   _____   7. hearts   _____

3. stomachs   _____   8. thumbs   _____

4. lungs   _____   9. livers   _____

5. noses   _____   10. eyes   _____

A CHOOSE THE CORRECT WORD

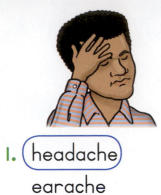

1. (headache)
   earache

2. stomachache
   backache

3. sunburn
   fever

4. rash
   insect bite

5. wart
   toothache

6. cough
   cavity

7. cold
   rash

8. sore throat
   stiff neck

9. the chills
   the hiccups

B LISTENING

Listen and circle the word you hear.

1. earache   (headache)

2. cold   cough

3. stomachache   backache

4. runny nose   bloody nose

5. fever   cavity

6. chills   hiccups

1. congested
   (dizzy)

2. cut
   twist

3. burn
   bruise

4. congested
   exhausted

5. cough
   sprain

6. scratch
   sneeze

D   **WORDSEARCH**

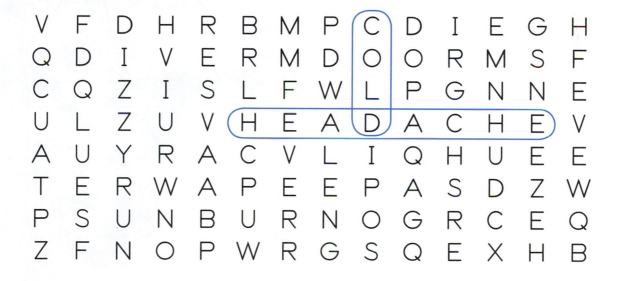

✔ COLD   __ FEVER   __ SNEEZE

__ DIZZY   ✔ HEADACHE   __ SUNBURN

A WHAT'S THE WORD?

1. b a n d a g e

2. _ _ _ _ _ _

3. _ _ _ _ _ _ _ _

4. _ _ _ _ _ _ _

5. _ _ _ _ _ _

6. _ _ _ _ _ _ _   _ _ _

B MATCHING: *First-Aid Supplies*

1. first-aid   ointment

2. adhesive   kit

3. antibiotic   peroxide

4. hydrogen   tape

5. non-aspirin   pain reliever

C MATCHING: *First-Aid Procedures*

1. He isn't breathing.   CPR

2. He's choking.   splint

3. She broke a finger.   Heimlich maneuver

4. He's bleeding.   rescue breathing

5. She doesn't have a pulse. tourniquet

A CHOOSE THE CORRECT WORD

1. fever
   (heatstroke)

2. the flu
   asthma

3. chicken pox
   measles

4. heart attack
   TB

5. asthma
   mumps

6. depression
   unconscious

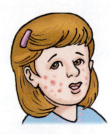

7. diabetes
   chicken pox

8. hypertension
   in shock

9. frostbite
   injured

B MATCHING

1. strep   infection

2. high blood   pox

3. heart   throat

4. ear   disease

5. chicken   pressure

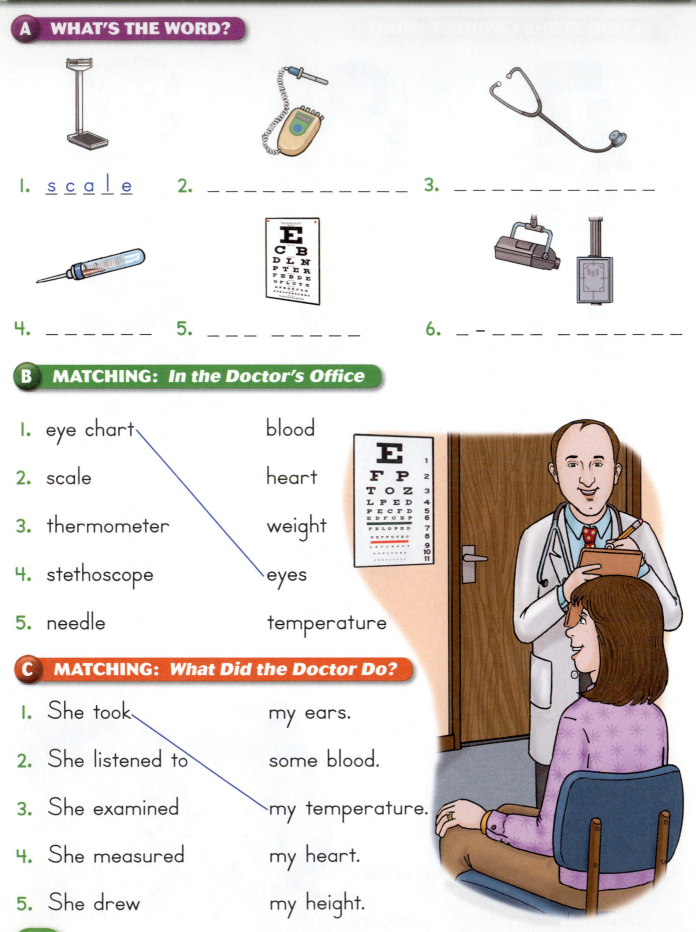

A **WHAT'S THE WORD?**

1. <u>s c a l e</u>

2. _ _ _ _ _ _ _ _ _ _ _

3. _ _ _ _ _ _ _ _ _ _ _

4. _ _ _ _ _ _ _

5. _ _ _   _ _ _ _ _

6. _ _ _ _ _   _ _ _ _ _ _ _ _

B **MATCHING: *In the Doctor's Office***

1. eye chart   blood

2. scale   heart

3. thermometer   weight

4. stethoscope   eyes

5. needle   temperature

C **MATCHING: *What Did the Doctor Do?***

1. She took   my ears.

2. She listened to   some blood.

3. She examined   my temperature.

4. She measured   my heart.

5. She drew   my height.

A CHOOSE THE CORRECT WORD

1. dentist
   (doctor)

2. nurse
   receptionist

3. filling
   stitches

4. cast
   mask

5. drill
   injection

6. brace
   sling

7. crutches
   braces

8. insurance card
   prescription

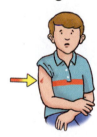

9. wound
   cavity

B MATCHING

1. medical history   room

2. examination   ball

3. dental   form

4. cotton   pack

5. ice   hygienist

A CHOOSE THE CORRECT WORD

1. (gargle)
   drink fluids

2. rest
   exercise

3. physical therapy
   acupuncture

4. air purifier
   vitamin

5. braces
   tests

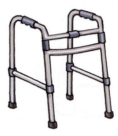

6. cane
   walker

7. heating pad
   humidifier

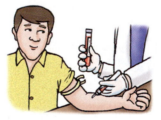

8. acupuncture
   blood work

9. counseling
   physical therapy

B MATCHING

1. drink   bed

2. rest in   vitamins

3. take   a specialist

4. go on   fluids

5. see   a diet

A **CHOOSE THE CORRECT WORD**

1. (aspirin)
   cough drops

2. nasal spray
   eye drops

3. cough syrup
   vitamins

4. throat lozenges
   antacid tablets

5. ointment
   cold tablets

6. cream
   decongestant

7. tablet
   capsule

8. pill
   caplet

9. teaspoon
   tablespoon

B **MATCHING**

1. cough   spray

2. throat   drops

3. nasal   lozenges

4. eye   tablets

5. antacid   syrup

A CHOOSE THE CORRECT WORD

1. gynecologist
   (pediatrician)

2. allergist
   cardiologist

3. orthopedist
   orthodontist

4. audiologist
   ENT specialist

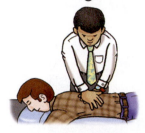

5. acupuncturist
   chiropractor

6. gerontologist
   orthodontist

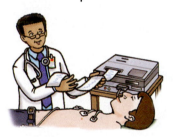

7. cardiologist
   gastroenterologist

8. ENT specialist
   ophthalmologist

9. counselor
   physical therapist

B MATCHING

1. eyes   gastroenterologist

2. heart   audiologist

3. ears   ophthalmologist

4. stomach   orthodontist

5. teeth   cardiologist

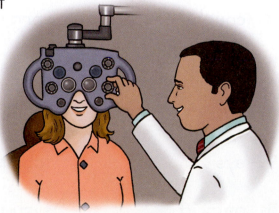

A CHOOSE THE CORRECT WORD

1. bed pan
   (hospital bed)

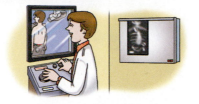

2. X-ray technician
   lab technician

3. waiting room
   operating room

4. dietitian
   obstetrician

5. medical chart
   monitor

6. I.V.
   EMT

7. surgeon
   radiologist

8. nurse's station
   laboratory

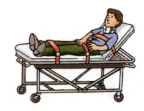

9. orderly
   gurney

B MATCHING

1. medical   pan
2. hospital   monitor
3. bed   gown
4. call   chart
5. vital signs   button

A WHAT IS IT?

1. <u>c o m b</u>

2. _ _ _ _ _ _

3. _ _ _ _ _ _ _ _ _ _

4. _ _ _ _ _ _ _ _

5. _ _ _ _ _ _ _ _ _

6. _ _ _ _ _ _ _ _ _

B WHICH GROUP?

blush	conditioner	lipstick	shampoo
brush	dental floss	mascara	toothbrush
comb	eyeliner	mouthwash	toothpaste

For teeth   For hair   For the face

_____   _____   _____blush_____

_____   _____   _____

_____   _____   _____

_____   _____   _____

C LISTENING

Listen. Write the correct number.

___ comb   ___ scissors   ___ shampoo

___ powder   _1_ hair brush   ___ toothpaste

114

A WHAT IS IT?

1. o i n t m e n t

2. _ _ _

3. _ _ _ _ _ _ _

4. _ _ _ _ _ _

5. _ _ _ _ _ _ _ _

6. _ _ _ _   _ _ _ _

B MATCHING

1. baby   swabs

2. diaper   powder

3. teething   ring

4. cotton   diapers

5. disposable   pins

C LISTENING

Listen. Write the number under the correct picture.

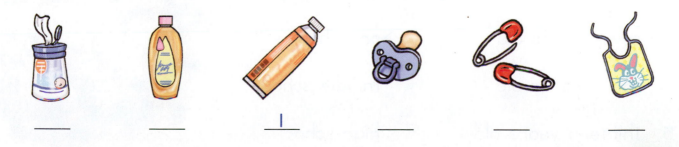

___   ___   1   ___   ___   ___

115

A CHOOSE THE CORRECT WORD

1. (college)
preschool

2. graduate school
middle school

3. trade school
nursery school

4. elementary school
adult school

5. junior high school
preschool

6. medical school
law school

B WHAT'S THE ORDER?

Number the schools from 1 (first) to 6 (last).

____ high school   ____ middle school

____ medical school   ____ college

__1__ nursery school   ____ elementary school

C MATCHING

1. four years old   adult school

2. sixteen years old   elementary school

3. seven years old   preschool

4. thirty years old   middle school

5. thirteen years old   high school

A WHERE ARE THEY?

1. The <u>p r i n c i p a l</u>

   is in the _ _ _ _ _ _.

2. The _ _ _ _ _ is in the

   _ _ _.

3. The _ _ _ _ _ _ _ _ _ _

   is in the _ _ _ _ _ _ _ _.

4. The _ _ _ _ _ is in the

   _ _ _ _ _ _ ' _ _ _ _ _ _.

5. The _ _ _ _ _ _ _ is in

   the _ _ _ _ _ _ _ _ _ _.

6. The _ _ _ _ _ _ _ _

   _ _ _ _ _ _ _ _ _ is in the

   _ _ _ _ _ _ _ _ _ _ _ _ _.

B DRAW A DIAGRAM

Draw a picture of your school. Show the different rooms and label them.

A WHAT'S THE SUBJECT?

1. h e a l t h

2. _ _ _ _ _

3. _ _ _

4. _ _ _ _ _ _ _

5. _ _ _ _ _ _ _ _ _

6. _ _ _ _ _ _

7. _ _ _ _ _ _

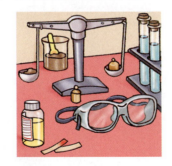

8. _ _ _ _ _ _ _ _ _ _

9. _ _ _ _ _ _ _ _ _

B WHICH GROUP?

| biology | chemistry | French | geography | history | Spanish |

Social Studies	Languages	Science
_____	_____	biology
_____	_____	_____

118

A WHAT'S THE ACTIVITY?

1. <u>c h o i r</u>

2. _ _ _ _ _

3. _ _ _ _ _ _ _ _ _

4. _ _ _ _ _

5. _ _ _ _ _ _ _ _ _ _

6. _ _ _ _ _ _ _ _

7. _ _ _ _ _ _
_ _ _ _ _ _ _ _

8. _ _ _ _ _ _ _ _ _ _
_ _ _ _ _ _ _

9. _ _ _ _ _ _ _
_ _ _ _ _ _ _ _ _

B WHICH GROUP?

band	chess	debate	newspaper	orchestra	yearbook

Music	Clubs	Writing
band	_____	_____
_____	_____	_____

119

A MATCHING

1. 3×2=6

2. 9-2=7

3. 8÷2=4

4. 1+4=5

subtraction

addition

multiplication

division

B MATCHING

1. minus   ×

2. times   +

3. equals   −

4. plus   ÷

5. divided by   =

C LISTENING

Listen and circle the answer.

1. +   −   ⊗   ÷

2. +   −   ×   ÷

3. +   −   ×   ÷

4. +   −   ×   ÷

5. +   −   ×   ÷

D WRITE THE MATH PROBLEMS

1. One plus six equals seven.   1 + 6 = 7

2. Eight divided by four is two.

3. Two times five equals ten.

4. Twelve minus seven is five.

E WHAT'S THE FRACTION?

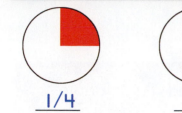

1/4   ___   ___   ___   ___

F MATCHING

1. one half   2/3

2. one quarter   3/4

3. two thirds   1/2

4. three fourths   1/3

5. one third   1/4

G LISTENING

Listen and circle the answer.

1. (1/3)   1/4

2. 1/4   1/2

3. 1/4   3/4

4. 1/4   3/4

5. 1/2   2/3

H WHAT'S THE PERCENT?

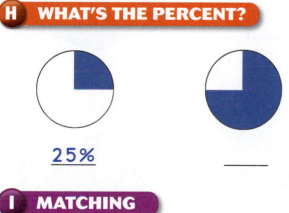

25%   ___   ___   ___

I MATCHING

1. fifty percent   25%

2. twenty-five percent   50%

3. one hundred percent   30%

4. thirty percent   75%

5. seventy-five percent   100%

J LISTENING

Listen and write the percent you hear.

1. __50%__   4. _____

2. _____   5. _____

3. _____   6. _____

A WHAT'S THE WORD?

line	cube	circle	sphere	pyramid	triangle
cone	angle	square	ellipse	cylinder	rectangle

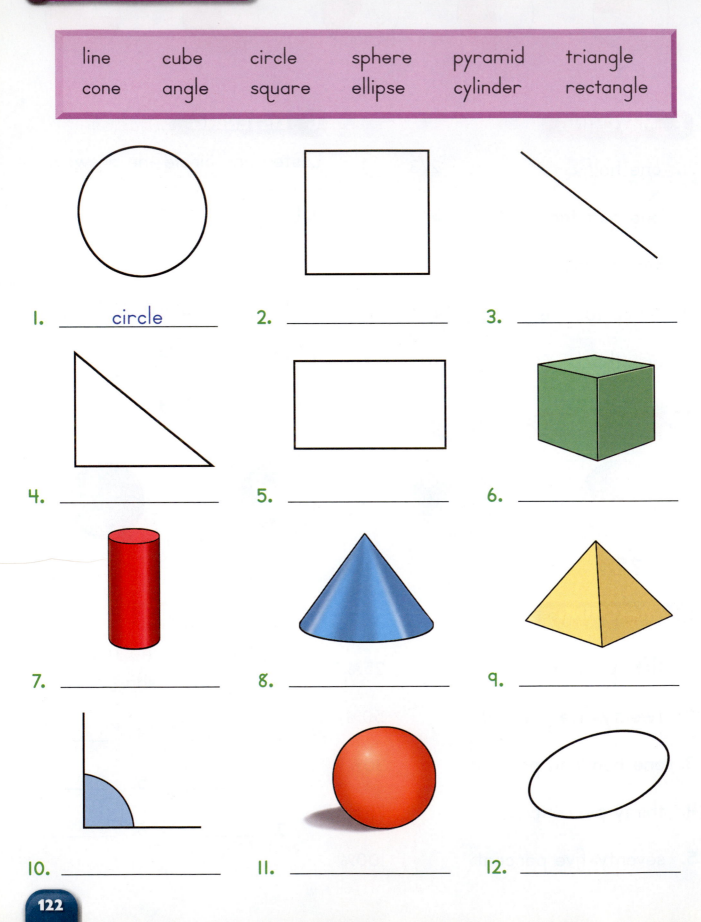

1. circle

2. _____

3. _____

4. _____

5. _____

6. _____

7. _____

8. _____

9. _____

10. _____

11. _____

12. _____

B WHICH GROUP?

| base | diameter | hypotenuse | length | radius | width |

Triangle	Circle	Rectangle
base	_____	_____
_____	_____	_____

C WHAT'S THE WORD?

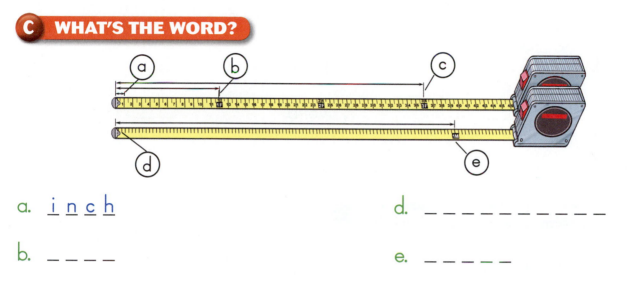

a. <u>i n c h</u>

b. _ _ _ _

c. _ _ _ _

d. _ _ _ _ _ _ _ _ _ _

e. _ _ _ _ _

D MATCHING: *Abbreviations*

1. cm   mile
2. m   yard
3. mi.   centimeter
4. km   foot
5. "   meter
6. '   inch
7. yd.   kilometer

E WHAT'S THE ANSWER?

1. 2.54 cm = __1__ "
2. 1' = ___ "
3. 0.914 m = 1 ___
4. 1.6 km = 1 ___
5. 1 yd. = ___ '
6. 0.305 m = ___ '

A WHAT'S THE PART OF SPEECH?

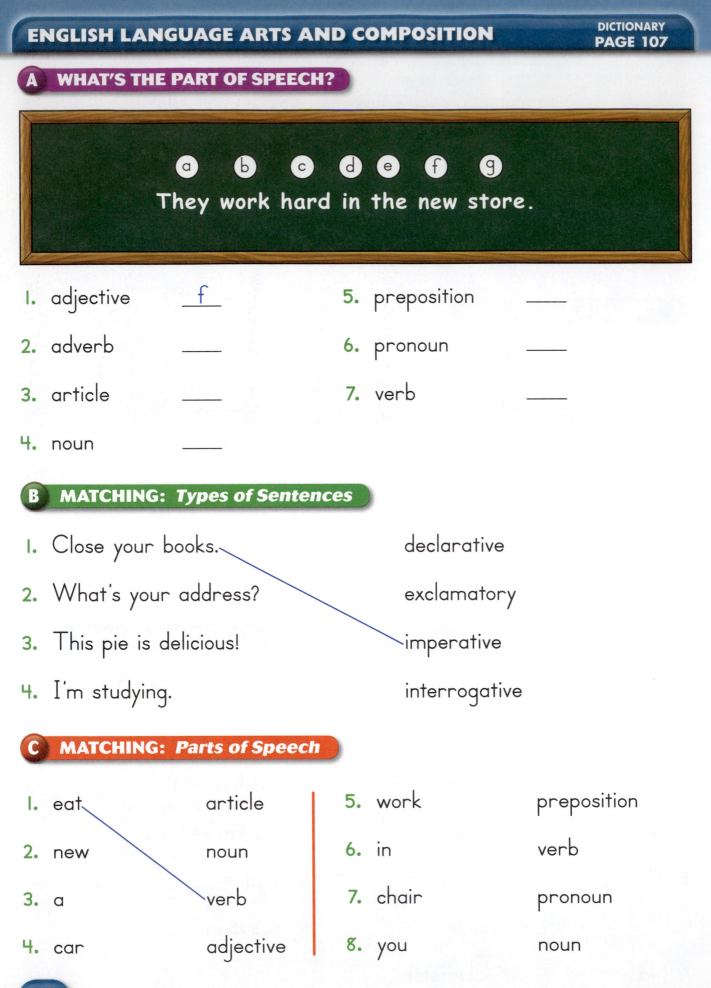

ⓐ ⓑ ⓒ ⓓ ⓔ ⓕ ⓖ
They work hard in the new store.

1. adjective _f_   5. preposition ____

2. adverb ____   6. pronoun ____

3. article ____   7. verb ____

4. noun ____

B MATCHING: *Types of Sentences*

1. Close your books.   declarative

2. What's your address?   exclamatory

3. This pie is delicious!   imperative

4. I'm studying.   interrogative

C MATCHING: *Parts of Speech*

1. eat   article   5. work   preposition

2. new   noun   6. in   verb

3. a   verb   7. chair   pronoun

4. car   adjective   8. you   noun

D MATCHING: *Punctuation Marks*

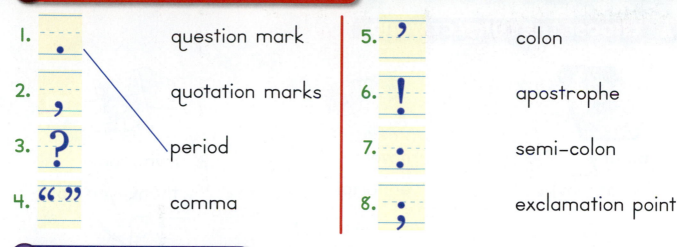

1. _____ •   question mark
2. _____ ,   quotation marks
3. ?   period
4. " "   comma

5. _____ '   colon
6. !   apostrophe
7. _____ :   semi-colon
8. _____ ;   exclamation point

E FIX THE SENTENCES

Write the correct punctuation mark.

> . ? ! , ' :

1. My sister's name is Berta.
2. What's your telephone number
3. These cookies are fantastic
4. Please get milk eggs, and bread at the supermarket.
5. My children are in elementary school
6. Our school has three music activities the band, the orchestra, and the choir.

F THE WRITING PROCESS

Choose the correct word.

1. Brainstorm (corrections   (ideas)).
2. Write a first (draft   declarative).
3. Make (edit   corrections).
4. Get (a title   feedback).
5. Write a (rewrite   final) copy.

A CHOOSE THE CORRECT WORD

1. poetry
   (biography)

2. novel
   editorial

3. invitation
   thank-you note

4. postcard
   poem

5. instant message
   note

6. e-mail
   letter

B MATCHING

1. Thank you for the book.

2. I was a very happy child.

3. It's beautiful here in Orlando!

4. Please come to our party.

5. I M FINE. HOW R U?

6. Crime in our city is a big problem.

invitation

editorial

instant message

postcard

thank-you note

autobiography

C WHICH GROUP?

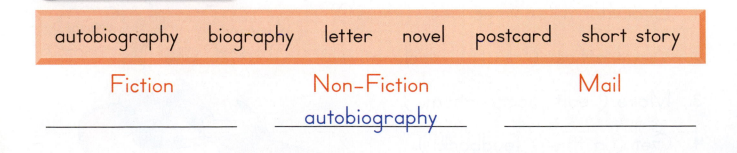

autobiography   biography   letter   novel   postcard   short story

Fiction	Non-Fiction	Mail
	autobiography	

A WHAT'S THE WORD?

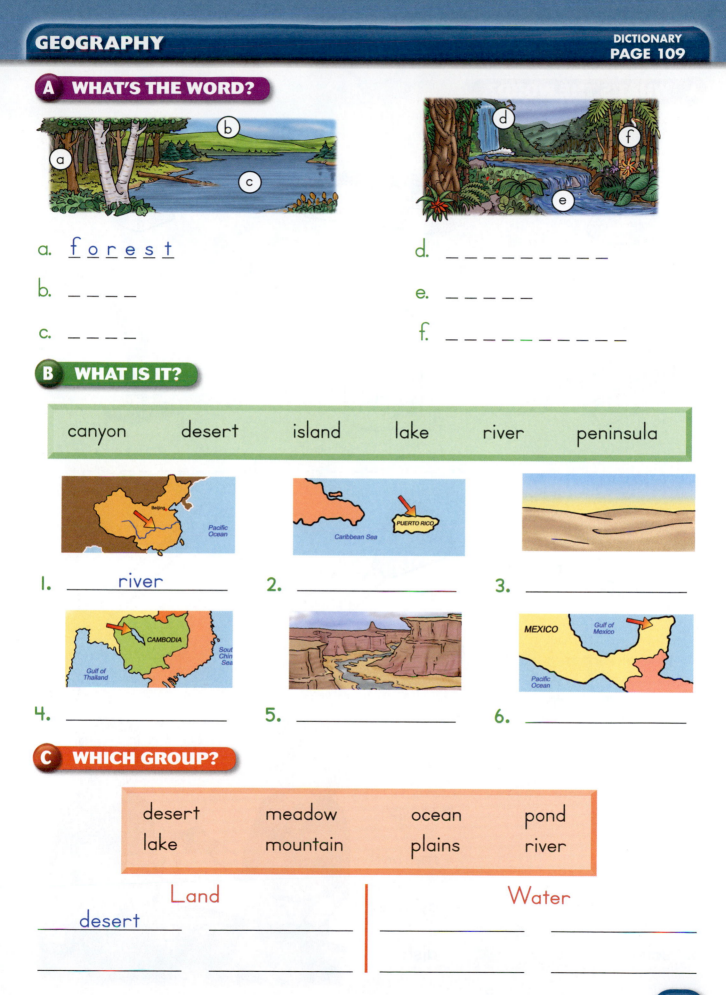

a. <u>f o r e s t</u>

b. _ _ _ _

c. _ _ _ _

d. _ _ _ _ _ _ _ _ _ _

e. _ _ _ _ _

f. _ _ _ _ _ _ _ _ _ _

B WHAT IS IT?

| canyon | desert | island | lake | river | peninsula |

1. _____ river _____

2. _____

3. _____

4. _____

5. _____

6. _____

C WHICH GROUP?

desert   meadow   ocean   pond
lake   mountain   plains   river

Land   Water

_____ desert _____   _____   _____   _____

_____   _____   _____   _____

A   WHAT'S THE WORD?

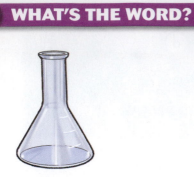

1. f l a s k

2. _ _ _ _ _ _

3. _ _ _ _ _ _

4. _ _ _ _ _ _

5. _ _ _ _ _ _

6. _ _ _ _ _ _ _ _ _ _

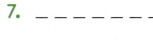

7. _ _ _ _ _ _ _

8. _ _ _ _ _ _ _

9. _ _ _ _   _ _ _ _

B   MATCHING

1. crucible — burner

2. petri   tongs

3. Bunsen   method

4. graduated   cylinder

5. scientific   dish

A WHAT'S THE WORD?

sun	moon	Earth	astronaut
star	comet	satellite	telescope

1. _moon_   2. _____   3. _____   4. _____

5. _____   6. _____   7. _____   8. _____

B WHAT'S MISSING?

1. M a r s   3. V _ n _ s   5. N e _ t _ _ e

2. E a r _ _   4. J _ p _ t _ r   6. M e _ c _ r y

C MATCHING

1. Big   saucer

2. solar   station

3. new   eclipse

4. space   Dipper

5. flying   moon

A WHAT'S THE OCCUPATION?

1. <u>c h e f</u>

2. _ _ _ _ _ _

3. _ _ _ _ _ _ _

4. _ _ _ _ _ _ _ _

5. _ _ _ _ _ _ _ _ _ _

6. _ _ _ _ _ _ _ _ _ _

7. _ _ _ _ _ _ _ _ _ _

8. _ _ _ _ _ _ _ _ _ _

9. _ _ _ _ _ _ _ _ _ _ _

10. _ _ _ _ _ _ _ _ _ _

11. _ _ _ _ _ _ _ _ _ _

12. _ _ _ _ _ _ _ _ _ _ _

B MATCHING: *What's the Job?*

1. construction   person
2. delivery   representative
3. home health   worker
4. data entry   aide
5. customer service   clerk

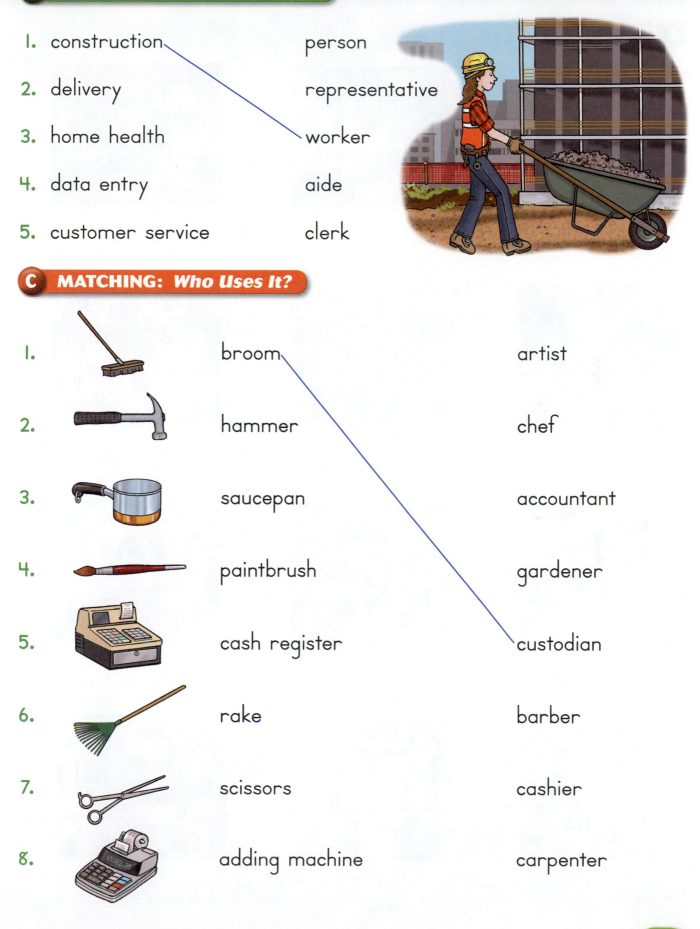

C MATCHING: *Who Uses It?*

1.	broom	artist
2.	hammer	chef
3.	saucepan	accountant
4.	paintbrush	gardener
5.	cash register	custodian
6.	rake	barber
7.	scissors	cashier
8.	adding machine	carpenter

131

A WHAT'S THE OCCUPATION?

1. <u>m o v e r</u>

2. _ _ _ _ _ _ _ _

3. _ _ _ _ _ _ _ _ _ _ _ _ _

4. _ _ _ _ _ _ _ _ _

5. _ _ _ _ _ _ _

6. _ _ _ _ _ _ _ _ _ _ _

7. _ _ _ _ _ _ _ _ _

8. _ _ _ _ _ _ _ _ _ _

9. _ _ _ _ _ _ _ _ _ _ _

10. _ _ _ _ _ _ _   11. _ _ _ _ _ _ _ _ _

12. _ _ _ _ _ _ _

MATCHING: *Who Works There?*

1. drug store
2. office
3. school
4. restaurant
5. store
6. garage

teacher
salesperson
waiter
mechanic
pharmacist
secretary

C **CROSSWORD**

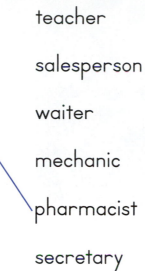

M E C H A N I C

ACROSS

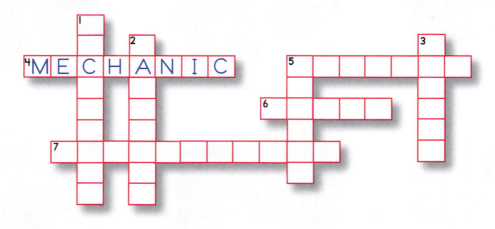

4.

5.

6.

7.

DOWN

1.

2.

3.

5.

133

A WHAT DO THEY DO?

1. s e w

2. _ _ _ _

3. _ _ _ _

4. _ _ _ _

5. _ _ _ _

6. _ _ _ _

7. _ _ _ _ _

8. _ _ _ _ _ _

9. _ _ _ _ _

10. _ _ _ _ _

11. _ _ _ _ _ _ _

12. _ _ _ _ _ _ _ _

1. Drivers   paint.

2. Actors   build things.

3. Bakers   drive.

4. Painters   assemble components.

5. Assemblers   clean.

6. Carpenters   act.

7. Housekeepers   bake.

1. I can guard   food.

2. I can serve   an airplane.

3. I can mow   the piano.

4. I can fly   buildings.

5. I can play   cars.

6. I can sell   lawns.

D JOURNAL: *My Work Skills*

I can _____

_____

_____.

A CHOOSE THE CORRECT WORD

1. form
   (sign)

2. note
   classified ad

3. job notice
   want ad

4. application
   resume

5. announcement
   interview

6. benefits
   salary

B MATCHING: Abbreviations

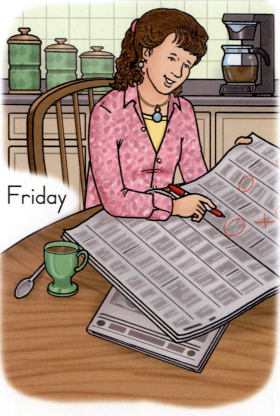

1. hr. ——— full-time
2. eves.   experience
3. FT   required
4. PT   hour
5. prev.   Monday through Friday
6. req.   available
7. exper.   evenings
8. avail.   previous
9. M-F   excellent
10. excel.   part-time

A WHAT'S THE WORD?

a. <u>c o a t r a c k</u>

b. _ _ _ _ _ _ _ _ _ _ _ _ _

c. _ _ _ _ _ _

d. _ _ _ _ _ _ _

e. _ _ _ _ _ _ _ _ _ _ _

f. _ _ _ _ _ _ _ _

g. _ _ _ _ _ _ _ _ _ _ _ _ _

h. _ _ _ _ _ _ _ _ _ _ _

B MATCHING

1. reception   cabinet

2. message   area

3. file   machine

4. employee   board

5. copy   lounge

A WHAT IS IT?

1. d e s k

2. _ _ _ _ _

3. _ _ _ _ _ _ _ _ _ _

4. _ _ _ _ _ _ _ _ _

5. _ _ _ _ _ _ _ _ _ _

6. _ _ _ _ _ _ _ _ _

7. _ _ _ _ _ _ _ _

8. _ _ _ _ _ _ _ _ _ _

9. _ _ _ _ _ _ _ _ _ _ _

B MATCHING

1. paper   tape

2. note   stick

3. rubber   folder

4. file   pad

5. glue   clip

6. packing   band

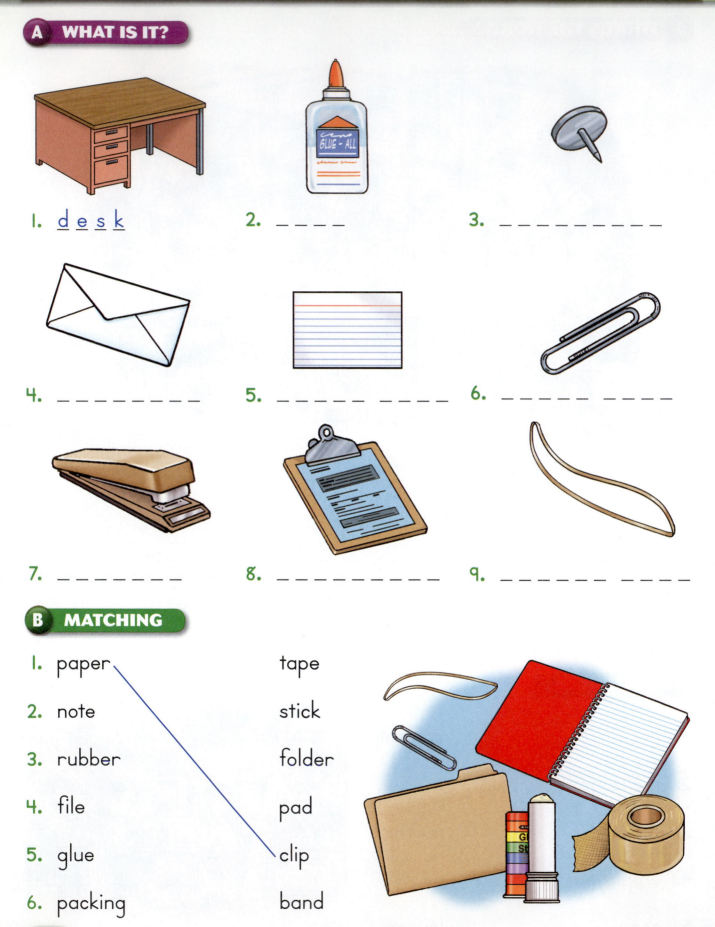

A CHOOSE THE CORRECT WORD

1. (time clock)
   work station

2. suggestion box
   dolly

3. line supervisor
   shipping clerk

4. packer
   forklift

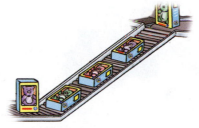

5. conveyor belt
   freight elevator

6. assembly line
   warehouse

7. loading dock
   shipping clerk

8. forklift
   hand truck

9. payroll office
   personnel office

B MATCHING

1. time   line

2. assembly   station

3. work   clock

4. suggestion   belt

5. conveyor   box

A WHAT'S THE WORD?

1. c r a n e

2. _ _ _ _ _ _ _

3. _ _ _ _ _ _ _ _ _

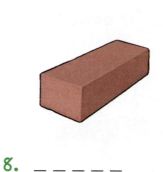

4. _ _ _ _

5. _ _ _ _ _ _ _ _

6. _ _ _ _ _ _ _ _ _

7. _ _ _ _ _

8. _ _ _ _ _ _

9. _ _ _ _ _ _ _ _ _ _ _ _

B WHICH GROUP?

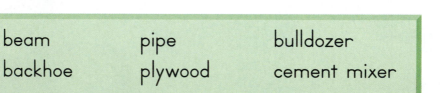

| beam | pipe | bulldozer |
| backhoe | plywood | cement mixer |

Materials   Machines

_____beam_____   _____

_____   _____

_____   _____

A WHAT'S THE WORD?

1. h e l m e t

2. _ _ _ _ _

3. _ _ _ _ _ _ _ _

  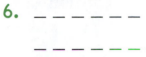

4. _ _ _ _ _ _ – _ _ _
   _ _ _

5. _ _ _ _
   _ _ _ _ _ _ _

6. _ _ _ _ _ _
   _ _ _ _ _ _

B MATCHING

1. hard hat   eyes

2. goggles   feet

3. mask   hands

4. safety boots   head

5. latex gloves   face

C LISTENING: *Warnings*

Listen and write the number under the correct picture.

___ ___ ___ ___ _1_ ___

A WHAT'S THE WORD?

taxi	ferry	bus stop	bus driver	bus
train	ticket	conductor	bus station	

1. _____bus_____

2. _____

3. _____

4. _____

5. _____

6. _____

7. _____

8. _____

9. _____

B MATCHING

1. ticket   compartment

2. bus   booth

3. fare   stop

4. luggage   counter

5. information   card

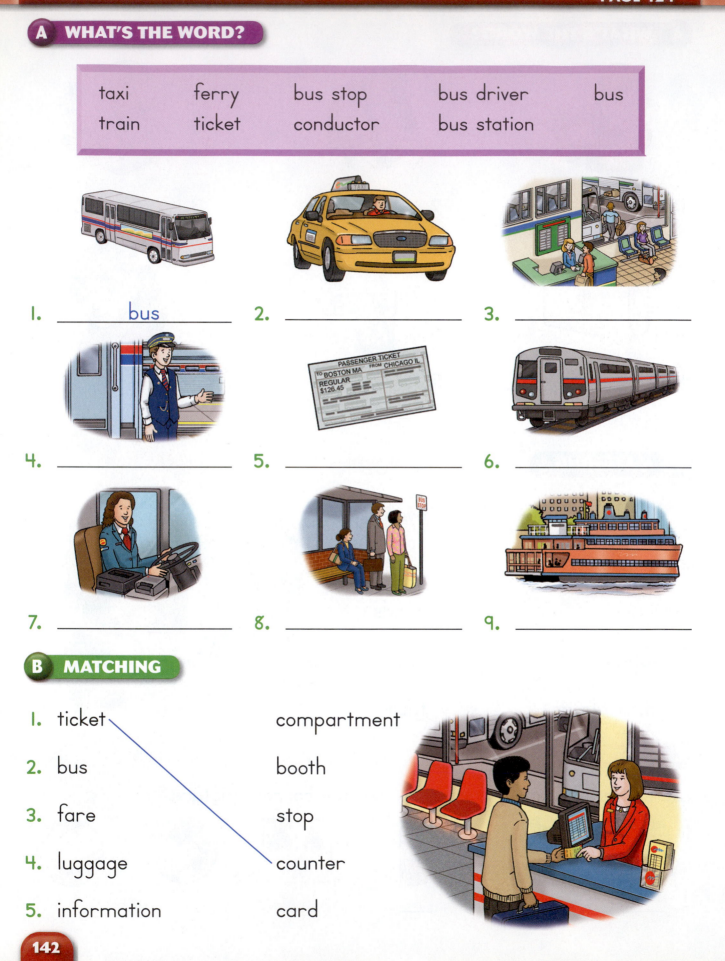

A WHAT'S THE WORD?

1. <u>s e d a n</u>

2. _ _ _ _ _

3. _ _ _ _ _ _ _ _ _ _

4. _ _ _

5. _ _ _ _ _ _ _

6. _ _ _ _ _ _ _ _ _ _

7. _ _ _ _ _ _
   _ _ _ _ _

8. _ _ _ _ _ _ _
   _ _ _

9. _ _ _ _ _ _ _
   _ _ _ _ _ _

B MATCHING

1. sports   wagon

2. motor   car

3. station   trailer

4. tractor   truck

5. pickup   scooter

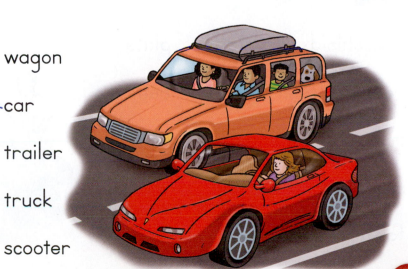

143

A WHAT'S THE WORD?

1. <u>t i r e</u>

2. _ _ _ _ _ _ _ _ _

3. _ _ _ _ _ _

4. _ _ _ _ _ _

5. _ _ _ _ _ _ _

6. _ _ _ _ _ _ _ _ _

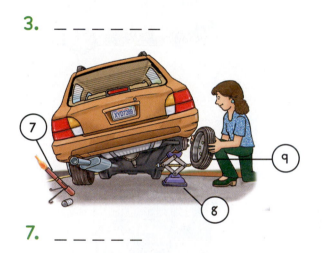

7. _ _ _ _ _ _

8. _ _ _ _

9. _ _ _ _ _ _ _ _ _

10. _ _ _ _ _ _ _

11. _ _ _ _ _ _

12. _ _ _ _ _ _

B MATCHING

1. windshield   plate

2. rear   belt

3. license   defroster

4. spark   wipers

5. fan   plugs

144

1. door lock
   seat belt

2. steering wheel
   clutch

3. ignition
   accelerator

4. gearshift
   turn signal

5. speedometer
   gas gauge

6. vent
   rearview mirror

7. radio
   horn

8. oil
   air

9. headrest
   air bag

D MATCHING

1. air   mirror

2. seat   bag

3. rearview   signal

4. turn   brake

5. emergency   belt

A WHAT'S THE WORD?

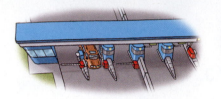  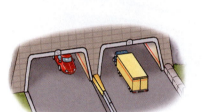

1. <u>t o l l b o o t h</u>　　2. _ _ _ _ _ _ _　　3. _ _ _ _ _ _ _ _ _ _ _

4. _ _ _ _ _ _ _ _ _　　5. _ _ _ _ _ _ _　　6. _ _ _ _ _ _ _ _ _ _ _ _ _

  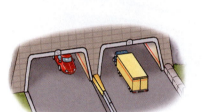

7. _ _ _ _ _ _
_ _ _ _　　8. _ _ _ _ _ _ _ _　　9. _ _ _ _ _ _ _ _ _ _ _ _ _

B MATCHING

1. speed limit　　　light

2. middle　　　　　highway

3. traffic　　　　　sign

4. interstate　　　　ramp

5. entrance　　　　lane

146

A   WHAT'S THE WORD?

| down | into | off | on | out of | over | under | up |

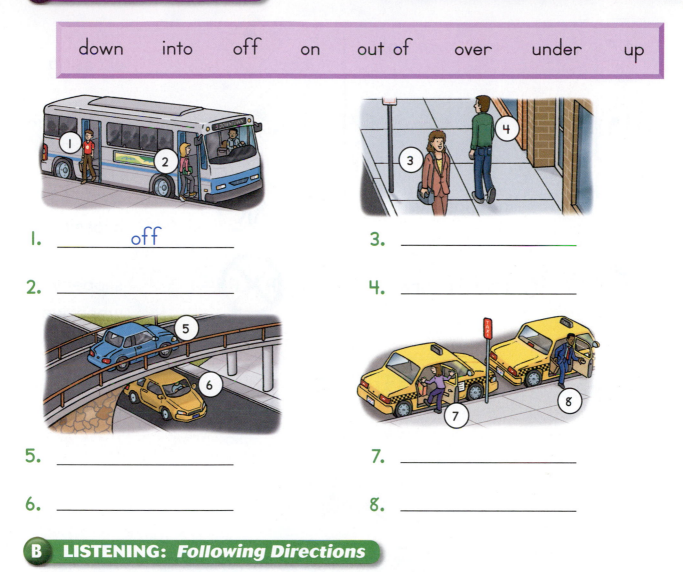

1. _____off_____

2. _____

3. _____

4. _____

5. _____

6. _____

7. _____

8. _____

B   LISTENING: *Following Directions*

Listen and write the number under the correct picture.

_____   _____   _____

_____   _____   ___1___

A MATCHING: *What's the Sign?*

1.  right turn only

2. no U-turn

3. no right turn

4. no left turn

5. school crossing

6. pedestrian crossing

7. railroad crossing

8. slippery when wet

B WHAT'S THE COMPASS DIRECTION?

_ _ _ _ _

w e s t 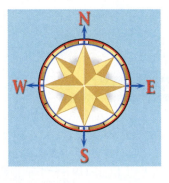 _ _ _ _

_ _ _ _ _

C LISTENING: *Traffic Signs*

Listen and write the number under the correct sign.

____   1   ____   ____   ____

A CHOOSE THE CORRECT WORD

1. gate
   (ticket)

2. suitcase
   garment bag

3. ticket agent
   customs officer

4. passport
   customs

5. visa
   boarding pass

6. security officer
   immigration officer

7. security checkpoint
   arrival and departure monitor

8. boarding area
   baggage claim area

B MATCHING

1. customs   counter

2. security   pass

3. ticket   checkpoint

4. boarding   detector

5. metal   officer

A   CHOOSE THE CORRECT WORD

1. (cockpit)
   control tower

2. terminal
   lavatory

3. life vest
   oxygen mask

4. aisle
   tray

5. conveyor belt
   seat belt

6. emergency exit
   boarding pass

B   MATCHING

1. emergency   bag

2. seat   exit

3. carry-on   belt

4. flight   compartment

5. overhead   mask

6. oxygen   sign

7. No Smoking   attendant

A WHAT'S THE WORD?

1. <u>f r o n t   d e s k</u>

3. _ _ _ _ _ _ _ _

2. _ _ _ _   _ _ _ _ _

4. _ _ _ _ _ _ _   _ _ _ _

5. _ _ _ _ _ _ _ _ _ _ _ _ _

7. _ _ _ _ _ _ _ _

6. _ _ _ _ _ _ _ _ _ _ _ _ _
   _ _ _ _

8. _ _ _ _ _ _ _
   _ _ _ _ _ _ _ _

B MATCHING

1. front   key

2. gift   desk

3. exercise   cart

4. room   room

5. housekeeping   shop

A CHOOSE THE CORRECT WORD

1. yarn
   (thread)

2. checkers
   chess

3. dice
   cards

4. pottery
   embroidery

5. photography
   astronomy

6. stamp album
   coin catalog

7. telescope
   binoculars

8. woodworking
   origami

9. knitting needle
   sewing machine

B MATCHING

1. camera   sewing

2. thread   painting

3. clay   photography

4. canvas   astronomy

5. telescope   pottery

A WHAT'S THE WORD?

1. <u>b e a c h</u>

2. _ _ _

3. _ _ _ _ _ _ _

4. _ _ _ _ _ _ _

5. _ _ _ _ _ _

6. _ _ _ _ _ _ _ _

7. _ _ _ _

8. _ _ _ _ _ _ _ _ _

9. _ _ _ _ _ _ _ _ _ _

B MATCHING

1. yard   market

2. flea   park

3. art   gallery

4. botanical   sale

5. amusement   gardens

153

A WHAT'S THE WORD?

ballfield	bike rack	sandbox	slide	trash can
bench	grill	seesaw	swings	

1. _____bench_____

2. _____

3. _____

4. _____

5. _____

6. _____

7. _____

8. _____

9. _____

B MATCHING

1. duck   can

2. trash   fountain

3. picnic   area

4. water   path

5. bike   pond

154

A CHOOSE THE CORRECT WORD

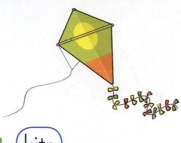

1. (kite)
   wave

2. pail
   shovel

3. sand castle
   snack bar

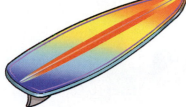

4. surfboard
   raft

5. shell
   rock

6. towel
   cooler

7. vendor
   surfer

8. sunscreen
   sun hat

9. lifeguard
   life preserver

B MATCHING

1. beach   stand

2. suntan   ball

3. life   lotion

4. lifeguard   bar

5. snack   preserver

155

A CHOOSE THE CORRECT WORD

1. (tent)
   rope

2. camping stove
   lantern

3. compass
   canteen

4. blanket
   sleeping bag

5. harness
   backpack

6. thermos
   hatchet

B WHAT'S THE WORD?

1. sleeping b a g

2. trail _ _ _

3. camping _ _ _ _ _

4. _ _ _ _ _ _ basket

5. _ _ _ _ stakes

6. _ _ _ _ _ _ boots

C MATCHING

1. camping   repellent

2. trail   bag

3. sleeping   stove

4. hiking   boots

5. insect   map

156

A CROSSWORD

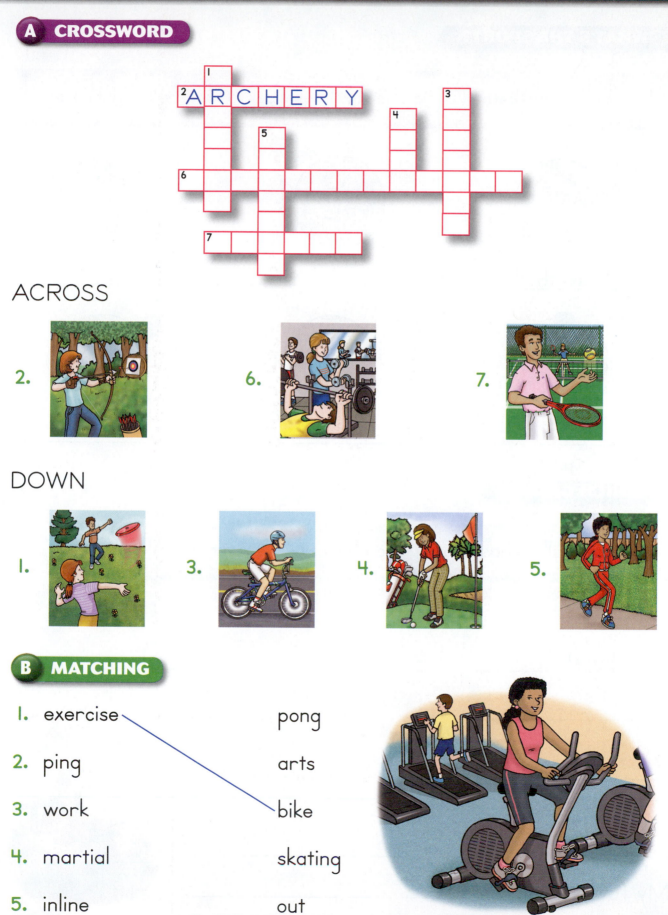

ACROSS

2.

6.

7.

DOWN

1.

3.

4.

5.

B MATCHING

1. exercise   pong

2. ping   arts

3. work   bike

4. martial   skating

5. inline   out

A WHAT'S THE SPORT?

| baseball | basketball | ice hockey | soccer | football | lacrosse |

1. _____basketball_____

2. _____

3. _____

4. _____

5. _____

6. _____

B WHICH GROUP?

| baseball | basketball | ice hockey | soccer | volleyball |

Field	Rink	Court
baseball		

C JOURNAL

My favorite sport is _____.

My favorite team is _____.

My favorite player is _____.

A WHAT'S THE WORD?

1. <u>b a s k e t b a l l</u>

2. _ _ _ _ _ _ _ _ _ _

3. _ _ _ _ _ _ _ _ _

4. _ _ _

5. _ _ _ _ _ _ _ _ _ _

6. _ _ _ _ _ _ _ _ _ _ _ _

7. _ _ _ _ _ _ _ _ _ _ _ _

8. _ _ _ _ _ _ _ _ _ _ _

B LISTENING

Listen. Write the number next to the correct picture.

A CHOOSE THE CORRECT WORD

1. (sled)
   bobsled

2. ski boots
   ice skates

3. poles
   bindings

4. bobsledding
   snowmobiling

5. bobsledding
   snowboarding

6. saucer
   bobsled

7. saucer
   blade

8. cross-country skiing
   downhill skiing

B MATCHING

1. skate   skiing

2. ice   dish

3. sledding   poles

4. downhill   guards

5. ski   skates

A WHAT'S THE WORD?

1. f i s h i n g

2. _ _ _ _ _ _ _

3. _ _ _ _ _ _ _

4. _ _ _ _ _ _ _ _

5. _ _ _ _ _ _ _

6. _ _ _ _ _ _ _ _ _

7. _ _ _ _ _ _ _ _

8. _ _ _ _ _ _ _ _

9. _ _ _ _ _ _ _ _ _

B MATCHING

1. rod   rowing

2. mask   swimming

3. oars   snorkeling

4. paddles   surfing

5. bathing suit   fishing

6. surfboard   canoeing

A CHOOSE THE CORRECT WORD

1. pass
   (kick)

2. hop
   stretch

3. reach
   bend

4. hit
   pitch

5. swing
   lift

6. dive
   dribble

7. serve
   skip

8. shoot
   bounce

9. push-up
   sit-up

10. somersault
    cartwheel

11. jumping jack
    deep knee bend

B LISTENING

Listen. Write the number under the correct picture.

___   ___   ___   ___ | ___

A WHAT'S THE WORD?

1. <u>a c t o r</u>

2. _ _ _ _ _ _ _ _

3. _ _ _ _ _ _ _ _ _

4. _ _ _ _ _ _ _ _

5. _ _ _ _ _ _ _ _ _

6. _ _ _ _ _ _   _ _ _ _ _ _

7. _ _ _ _ _   _ _ _ _ _ _

8. _ _ _ _ _   _ _ _ _ _ _

B MATCHING

1. singer   comedy club

2. ballerina   orchestra

3. conductor   music club

4. comedian   play

5. actor   ballet

A CHOOSE THE CORRECT WORD

1. (jazz)
   folk music

2. bluegrass
   rock music

3. musical
   drama

4. cartoon
   drama

5. western
   comedy

6. talk show
   game show

B LISTENING

Listen. Write the number next to the type of music you hear.

___ classical   ___ jazz   ___ reggae   _1_ rap music

___ gospel   ___ country   ___ rock

C JOURNAL

My favorite TV show is _____.

My favorite movie is _____.

My favorite movie star is _____.

My favorite type of music is _____.

A CHOOSE THE CORRECT WORD

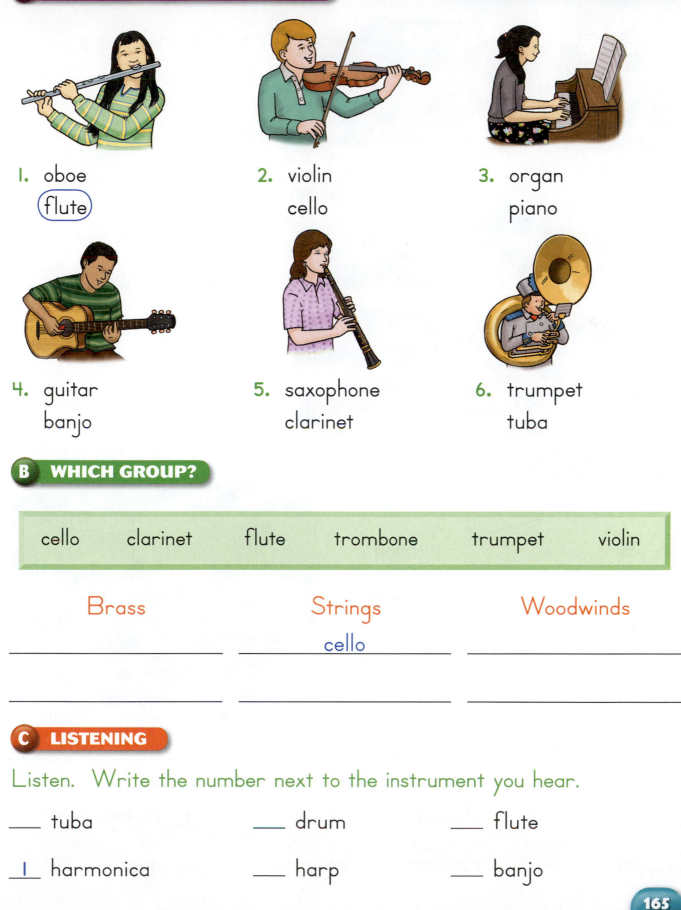

1. oboe
   (flute)

2. violin
   cello

3. organ
   piano

4. guitar
   banjo

5. saxophone
   clarinet

6. trumpet
   tuba

B WHICH GROUP?

| cello | clarinet | flute | trombone | trumpet | violin |

Brass	Strings	Woodwinds
	cello	

C LISTENING

Listen. Write the number next to the instrument you hear.

___ tuba   ___ drum   ___ flute

_1_ harmonica   ___ harp   ___ banjo

A WHAT'S THE WORD?

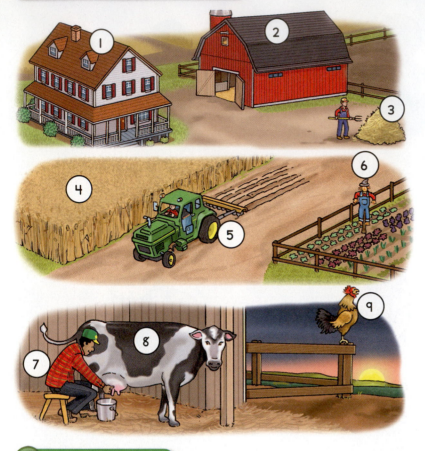

1. <u>f a r m h o u s e</u>
2. _ _ _ _
3. _ _ _
4. _ _ _ _ _
5. _ _ _ _ _ _
6. _ _ _ _ _ _ _ _
7. _ _ _ _ _ _
8. _ _ _
9. _ _ _ _ _ _

B MATCHING

1. hired   coop
2. pig   hand
3. chicken   garden
4. irrigation   pen
5. vegetable   system

C LISTENING

Listen. Write the number next to the farm animal you hear.

___ horse   ___ chicken   ___ pig   _1_ turkey

___ lamb   ___ rooster   ___ cow   ___ goat

A WHAT'S THE WORD?

bat	bear	camel	skunk	rabbit	squirrel
fox	deer	mouse	horse	monkey	elephant

1. _____deer_____

2. _____

3. _____

4. _____

5. _____

6. _____

7. _____

8. _____

9. _____

10. _____

11. _____

12. _____

B LISTENING

Listen. Write the number next to the animal or pet you hear.

___ donkey   ___ bear   ___ dog   ___ hyena

___ mouse   ___ cat   _1_ lion   ___ elephant

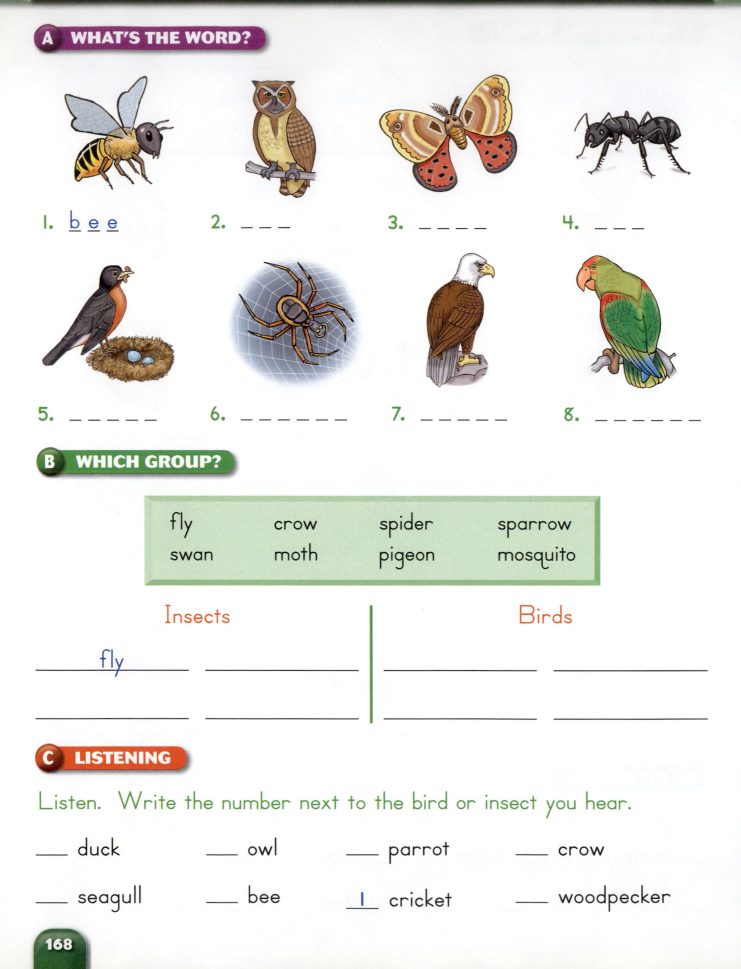

A WHAT'S THE WORD?

1. b e e

2. _ _ _

3. _ _ _ _

4. _ _ _

5. _ _ _ _ _

6. _ _ _ _ _ _

7. _ _ _ _ _

8. _ _ _ _ _ _

B WHICH GROUP?

| fly | crow | spider | sparrow |
| swan | moth | pigeon | mosquito |

Insects | Birds

fly _____   _____ | _____   _____

_____   _____ | _____   _____

C LISTENING

Listen. Write the number next to the bird or insect you hear.

___ duck   ___ owl   ___ parrot   ___ crow

___ seagull   ___ bee   _1_ cricket   ___ woodpecker

A   WHAT'S THE WORD?

crab	snake	turtle	alligator	seal
frog	whale	dolphin	jellyfish	

1. _____seal_____

2. _____

3. _____

4. _____

5. _____

6. _____

7. _____

8. _____

9. _____

B   WHICH GROUP?

cobra	flounder	seal	snake	tuna	whale

Fish	Sea Animals	Reptiles
		cobra
_____	_____	_____
_____	_____	_____

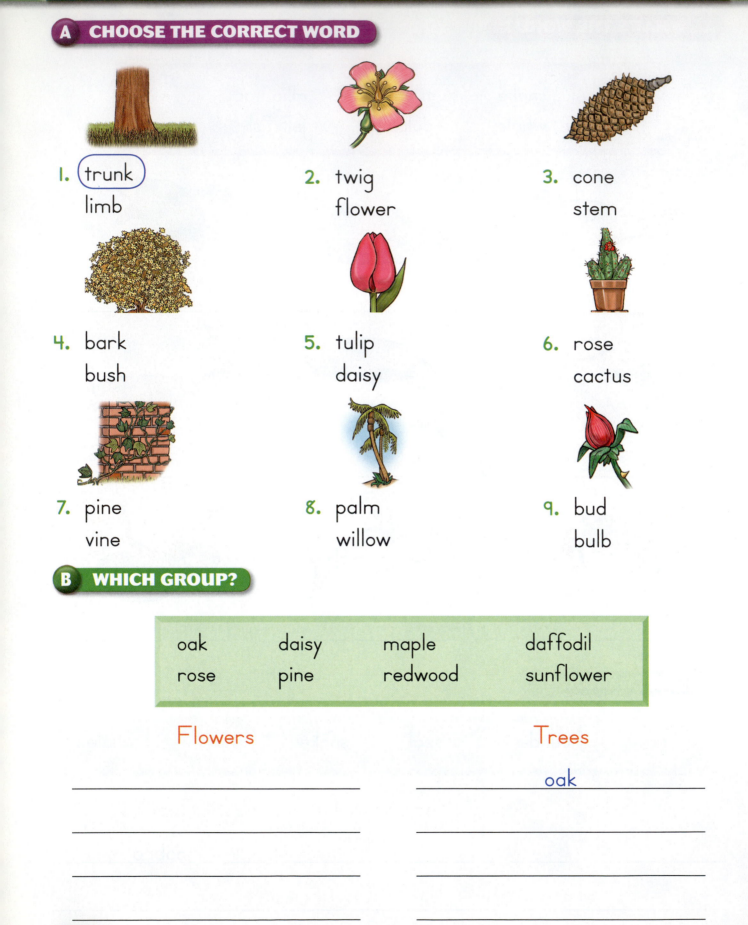

A CHOOSE THE CORRECT WORD

1. (trunk)
   limb

2. twig
   flower

3. cone
   stem

4. bark
   bush

5. tulip
   daisy

6. rose
   cactus

7. pine
   vine

8. palm
   willow

9. bud
   bulb

B WHICH GROUP?

| oak | daisy | maple | daffodil |
| rose | pine | redwood | sunflower |

Flowers   Trees

                                           oak

_____   _____

_____   _____

_____   _____

_____   _____

A WHAT'S THE WORD?

1. <u>o i l</u>

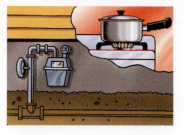

2. _ _ _

3. _ _ _ _ _

4. _ _ _ _

5. _ _ _ _ _ _ _ _ _

6. _ _ _ _ _ _ _

7. _ _ _ _ _

_ _ _ _ _ _ _ _ _

8. _ _ _ _ _ _

_ _ _ _ _ _

9. _ _ _ _ _ _ _ _ _ _ _

_ _ _ _ _ _

B MATCHING

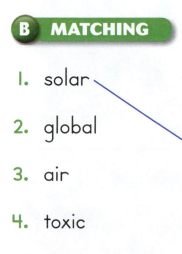

1. solar   warming

2. global   waste

3. air   energy

4. toxic   rain

5. acid   pollution

A WHAT'S THE WORD?

1. <u>t o r n a d o</u>

2. _ _ _ _ _

3. _ _ _ _ _ _ _ _

4. _ _ _ _ _ _ _

5. _ _ _ _ _ _ _

6. _ _ _ _ _ _ _ _

7. _ _ _ _ _ _ _ _

8. _ _ _ _ _ _ _ _ _

9. _ _ _ _ _ _ _ _ _ _

B MATCHING

1. fire
2. big waves
3. snow and wind
4. wind and rain
5. no rain

hurricane
wildfire
drought
blizzard
tsunami

ANSWER KEY AND LISTENING SCRIPTS

WORKBOOK PAGES 1–3

A. CIRCLE THE SAME WORD
1. NAME   3. STATE   5. ADDRESS
2. CITY   4. STREET

B. MATCHING
1. CA
2. 90036
3. GARDEN STREET
4. 323-524-3278
5. GLORIA SANCHEZ
6. 227-93-6185

F. LISTENING

Listen and circle the words you hear.

1. A. What's your name?
   B. My name? John.
2. A. What's your zip code?
   B. My zip code? 22315.
3. A. What's your social security number?
   B. My social security number? 976-24-3069.
4. A. What's your street?
   B. My street? North Tenth Street.
5. A. What's your city?
   B. My city? Sacramento.
6. A. What's your first name?
   B. My first name? Ana.

Answers
1. name   4. street
2. zip code   5. city
3. social security   6. first

WORKBOOK PAGES 4–5

A. WHO ARE THEY?
1. b   3. f   5. c
2. d   4. e   6. a

B. MATCHING
1. father   4. mother
2. sister   5. son
3. brother   6. daughter

C. WHAT'S MISSING?
1. wife   4. grandson
   sister   brother
2. father   5. baby
   mother   daughter
3. husband   6. grandmother
   son   grandfather

D. WHICH GROUP?

Parents	Children
1. father	5. son
2. mother	6. daughter
3. husband	7. brother
4. wife	8. sister

WORKBOOK PAGES 6–7

A. WHO ARE THEY?
1. d   2. a   3. c   4. e   5. b

B. WHAT'S MISSING?
1. aunt   2. nephew
   uncle   niece

3. cousin   5. mother-in-law
   uncle   father-in-law
4. son-in-law 6. sister-in-law
   sister-in-law   brother-in-law

C. WHICH GROUP?
nephew   cousin   aunt
uncle   niece

D. WHO ARE THEY?
1. uncle   5. father
2. aunt   6. aunt
3. nephew   7. uncle
4. niece   8. sister

WORKBOOK PAGES 8–9

A. WHAT'S THE WORD?
a. map   g. globe
b. teacher   h. board
c. book   i. desk
d. pencil   j. notebook
e. bookcase   k. student
f. clock   l. ruler

B. LISTENING

Listen and circle the word you hear.

1. A. Where's the pencil?
   B. The pencil? It's on the desk.
2. A. Where's the paper?
   B. The paper? It's on the bookshelf.
3. A. Where's the chalk?
   B. The chalk? It's on the teacher's desk.
4. A. Where's the ruler?
   B. The ruler? It's on my desk.
5. A. Where's your notebook?
   B. My notebook? It's on my desk.
6. A. Where's the computer?
   B. The computer? It's on the table.

Answers
1. pencil   4. ruler
2. paper   5. notebook
3. chalk   6. computer

C. WHAT'S IN THE CLASSROOM?
1. globe   4. computer
2. map   5. wastebasket
3. book

WORKBOOK PAGES 10–11

A. LISTENING

Listen. Put a check under the correct picture.

1. A. Please write your name.
   B. Write my name? Sure.
2. A. Please close your book.
   B. Close my book? Sure.
3. A. Please help each other.
   B. Help each other? Okay.
4. A. Please hand in your homework.
   B. Hand in my homework? Okay.
5. A. Please answer the questions.
   B. Answer the questions? Okay.
6. A. Please turn off the lights.
   B. Turn off the lights? Sure.

Answers
1. ✓ _____
2. _____ ✓
3. ✓ _____
4. ✓ _____
5. ✓ _____
6. _____ ✓

B. MATCHING
1. your book.   4. down.
2. your name.   5. the board.
3. up.

C. WHAT'S THE ACTION?
1. Write   5. Do
2. Close   6. Circle
3. Raise   7. Work
4. Go   8. Turn off

WORKBOOK PAGES 12–13

A. CHOOSE THE CORRECT ANSWER
1. above   3. between   5. front
2. left   4. right   6. under

B. WHERE ARE THEY?
1. above   5. under
2. on   6. behind
3. in front of   7. right
4. next to

WORKBOOK PAGES 14–15

A. MATCHING
1. get up   4. eat lunch
2. take a shower   5. go to bed
3. brush my teeth   6. comb my hair

B. WHAT DO YOU DO EVERY DAY?
1. wash   3. shave   5. eat
2. make   4. brush   6. sleep

C. LISTENING

Listen. Write the correct number.

1. (Sound: bath)
2. (Sound: shower)
3. (Sound: making dinner)
4. (Sound: brushing teeth)
5. (Sound: electric shaver)

Answers
2   3
4   5
1

WORKBOOK PAGES 16–17

A. LISTENING

Listen. Put a check under the correct picture.

1. A. What's your father doing?
   B. He's washing the dishes.
   A. Washing the dishes?
   B. Yes.
2. A. What's your sister doing?
   B. She's studying.
   A. Studying?
   B. Yes.
3. A. What's your cousin doing?
   B. She's working.
   A. Working?
   B. Yes.

4. A. What's your son doing?
   B. He's walking the dog.
   A. Walking the dog?
   B. Yes.
5. A. What's your brother doing?
   B. He's driving to work.
   A. Driving to work?
   B. Yes.
6. A. What's your wife doing?
   B. She's feeding the cat.
   A. Feeding the cat?
   B. Yes.

Answers

1. ✓ ___
2. ___ ✓
3. ✓ ___
4. ___ ✓
5. ___ ✓
6. ✓ ___

B. MATCHING

1. the cat   3. the dishes
2. work   4. home

C. WHAT DO YOU DO EVERY DAY?

1. work   3. clean   5. iron
2. drive   4. study

D. LISTENING: *What Are They Doing?*

Listen. Write the correct number.

1. (Sound: driving to work)
2. (Sound: washing machine)
3. (Sound: washing dishes)
4. (Sound: vacuum)
5. (Sound: feeding baby)

Answers

5   3
4   2
1

WORKBOOK PAGES 18–19

A. MATCHING

1. listening to the radio
2. practicing the piano
3. reading the newspaper
4. playing basketball
5. swimming
6. exercising

B. WHAT ARE YOU DOING?

1. watching   4. writing
2. playing   5. reading
3. planting   6. listening

C. LISTENING: *What Are They Doing?*

Listen. Write the correct number.

1. (Sound: playing the piano)
2. (Sound: playing the guitar)
3. (Sound: swimming)
4. (Sound: exercising)
5. (Sound: playing basketball)
6. (Sound: using the computer)

Answers

4   1
3   5
6   2

WORKBOOK PAGES 20–21

A. WHAT'S THE WORD?

1. morning   4. new
2. afternoon   5. soon
3. thanks   6. night

B. MATCHING

1. afternoon.   4. new?
2. you?   5. later.
3. thanks.

C. WHAT'S THE WORD?

1. Hello, Hi
2. speak, sorry
3. introduce, meet

D. MATCHING

1. understand.   4. repeat that?
2. me.   5. a question?
3. you.

WORKBOOK PAGES 22–23

A. WHAT'S THE WEATHER?

1. sunny   6. snowing
2. cloudy   7. windy
3. raining   8. smoggy
4. humid   9. lightning
5. foggy

B. LISTENING: *What's the Weather Forecast?*

Listen and circle the weather you hear.

1. It's snowing today.
2. It's windy today.
3. It's going to be cloudy tomorrow.
4. It's going to be foggy tomorrow.
5. It's drizzling today.
6. There's going to be a thunderstorm this afternoon.

Answers

1. snowing   4. foggy
2. windy   5. drizzling
3. cloudy   6. thunderstorm

C. HOW'S THE WEATHER?

1. hot   4. warm
2. cool   5. cold
3. freezing

D. WORDSEARCH

```
B D Z Z T Y S F C L E A R G
F O G G Y L U I L D M U N C
I F J R K S N O W I N G X L
A R E S G B N T H U V C G O
H Q P B J L Y Q U Q W S O U
W Y H U M I D A L K V O P D
A M H P F X E T M W I N D Y
R A I N I N G C R K W E N X
M D O X W I A S Y V C N J Z
```

WORKBOOK PAGES 24–25

A. MATCHING

1. six, 6   4. three, 3
2. eight, 8   5. five, 5
3. seven, 7

B. WHAT'S THE NUMBER?

1. 9   2. 4   3. 16   4. 12   5. 50

C. WHAT'S THE WORD?

four
six
thirteen
seventy
one hundred

D. LISTENING

Listen and circle the number you hear.

1. A. How old is your daughter?
   B. She's thirteen years old.
   A. Thirteen?
   B. Yes.
2. A. How old is your son?
   B. He's forty years old.
   A. Forty?
   B. Yes.
3. A. How old is he?
   B. He's seventy years old.
   A. Seventy?
   B. Yes.
4. A. How old is she?
   B. She's sixteen years old.
   A. Sixteen?
   B. Yes.
5. A. How old are you?
   B. I'm twenty-four years old.
   A. Twenty-four?
   B. Yes.
6. A. How old are you?
   B. I'm thirty-five years old.
   A. Thirty-five?
   B. Yes.

Answers

1. 13   3. 70   5. 24
2. 40   4. 16   6. 35

E. MATCHING

1. 3rd   6. 11th
2. 9th   7. 8th
3. 1st   8. 4th
4. 12th   9. 80th
5. 60th   10. 14th

F. WHAT'S THE NUMBER?

1. 2nd   4. 1st
2. 10th   5. 50th
3. 13th   6. 3rd

G. WHAT'S THE WORD?

fourteenth
sixth
sixtieth
eleventh
twentieth
twenty-first

H. MATCHING

1. fourth   4. first
2. fifth   5. third
3. second   6. tenth

I. LISTENING

Listen and circle the number you hear.

1. A. What floor do you live on?
   B. I live on the fourteenth floor.
   A. The fourteenth?
   B. Yes.

2. A. What floor do you live on?
   B. I live on the seventh floor.
   A. The seventh?
   B. Yes.
3. A. What floor do you live on?
   B. I live on the thirtieth floor.
   A. The thirtieth?
   B. Yes.
4. A. What floor do you live on?
   B. The eighteenth floor.
   A. The eighteenth?
   B. Yes.
5. A. What floor do you live on?
   B. The twenty-second floor.
   A. The twenty-second?
   B. Yes.

Answers

1. 14th   4. 18th
2. 7th   5. 22nd
3. 30th

WORKBOOK PAGES 26–27

A. WHAT TIME IS IT?

| 10:00 | 3:30 | 1:15 | 6:45 |
| 7:20 | 8:05 | 12:55 | 4:40 |

B. CHOOSE THE CORRECT ANSWER

1. a   3. a
2. b   4. b

C. MATCHING

1. 5:45, five forty-five
2. 6:20, twenty after six
3. 6:30, six thirty
4. 6:15, six fifteen
5. 6:50, ten to seven

D. CHOOSE THE CORRECT TIME

1. 7:00 A.M.   3. noon
2. midnight   4. 10:00 P.M.

E. LISTENING

Listen and circle the time you hear.

1. A. What time does the train leave?
   B. At eight thirty.
   A. Eight thirty? Thanks.
2. A. What time does the train leave?
   B. At ten o'clock.
   A. Ten o'clock? Thanks.
3. A. When does the bus leave?
   B. At three fifteen.
   A. Three fifteen? Thanks.
4. A. When does the bus leave?
   B. At six forty-five.
   A. Six forty-five? Thanks.
5. A. When will we arrive?
   B. At half past one.
   A. Half past one? Thanks.
6. A. When will we arrive?
   B. At one oh five.
   A. One oh five? Thanks.

Answers

1. 8:30   4. 6:45
2. 10:00   5. 1:30
3. 3:15   6. 1:05

WORKBOOK PAGES 28–29

A. WHAT IS IT?

1. penny, 1¢, $.01
2. dime, 10¢, $.10
3. quarter, 25¢, $.25
4. nickel, 5¢, $.05
5. half dollar, 50¢, $.50

B. WHAT'S THE AMOUNT?

1. $.05   5. $.26
2. $.15   6. $.25
3. $.40   7. $.75
4. $.12   8. $1.00

C. MATCHING

1. ten dollars, $10.00
2. one dollar, $1.00
3. fifty dollars, $50.00
4. five dollars, $5.00
5. twenty dollars, $20.00

D. WHAT'S THE AMOUNT?

1. $11.00   3. $30.00
2. $15.00   4. $10.00

E. LISTENING

Listen and circle the amount you hear.

1. A. How much is this?
   B. Thirty-five dollars.
   A. Thirty-five dollars?
   B. Yes.
2. A. How much is this?
   B. Five dollars.
   A. Five dollars?
   B. Yes.
3. A. How much is this?
   B. Forty-four cents.
   A. Forty-four cents?
   B. Yes.
4. A. How much is this?
   B. Sixty-one dollars.
   A. Sixty-one dollars?
   B. Yes.
5. A. How much is this?
   B. Seven dollars and ten cents.
   A. Seven dollars and ten cents?
   B. Yes.
6. A. How much is this?
   B. Forty-one dollars and fourteen cents.
   A. Forty-one dollars and fourteen cents?
   B. Yes.

Answers

1. $35.00   4. $61.00
2. $5.00   5. $7.10
3. $.44   6. $41.14

WORKBOOK PAGES 30–31

A. WHAT'S MISSING?

1. January   7. July
2. February   8. August
3. March   9. September
4. April   10. October
5. May   11. November
6. June   12. December

B. WRITE THE MONTH

1. February   4. September
2. May   5. December
3. July

C. WHAT'S MISSING?

1. Sunday   5. Thursday
2. Monday   6. Friday
3. Tuesday   7. Saturday
4. Wednesday

D. WRITE THE DAY

1. Sunday   5. Thursday
2. Monday   6. Friday
3. Tuesday   7. Saturday
4. Wednesday

E. MATCHING

1. June 14, 2008
2. April 6, 1990
3. January 2, 2009
4. February 1, 2009
5. March 6, 2000

G. LISTENING

Listen and circle the correct answer.

1. A. What day is it?
   B. It's Monday.
   A. Monday? Thanks.
2. A. What day is it?
   B. It's Tuesday.
   A. Tuesday? Thanks.
3. A. What month is it?
   B. June.
   A. June? Thanks.
4. A. What month is it?
   B. It's December.
   A. December? Thanks.
5. A. What's today's date?
   B. Today is April fourth.
   A. April fourth? Thanks.
6. A. When is your birthday?
   B. My birthday is on March seventh.
   A. March seventh?
   B. Yes.

Answers

1. Monday   4. December
2. Tuesday   5. April 4
3. June   6. March 7

WORKBOOK PAGE 32

A. WHAT'S THE WORD?

1. Today   4. this
2. Yesterday   5. last
3. Tomorrow   6. next

C. WHAT'S THE SEASON?

1. summer   3. fall
2. winter   4. spring

WORKBOOK PAGE 33

A. CHOOSE THE CORRECT ANSWER

1. b   2. a   3. b   4. a

B. WHAT TYPE OF HOUSING?

1. house   4. dormitory
2. apartment   5. townhouse
3. duplex   6. shelter

WORKBOOK PAGES 34–35

A. CIRCLE THE CORRECT WORD
1. bookcase
2. armchair
3. rug
4. floor
5. painting
6. DVD player

B. WHERE IS IT?
1. lamp
2. pillow
3. drapes
4. plant
5. painting

C. WHAT'S THE WORD?
1. rug
2. sofa
3. lamp
4. plant
5. window
6. bookcase
7. pillow
8. fireplace
9. television

WORKBOOK PAGES 36–37

A. WHAT'S IN THE DINING ROOM?
1. table
2. chair
3. candle
4. teapot
5. pitcher
6. plate

B. MATCHING
1. cabinet
2. shaker
3. dish
4. bowl
5. pot

C. LISTENING
Listen and circle the words you hear.

1. A. Please pass the butter dish.
   B. The butter dish? Here you are.
2. A. Please pass the pitcher.
   B. The pitcher? Here you are.
3. A. May I have the salt shaker, please?
   B. The salt shaker? Here you are.
4. A. I really like your tablecloth.
   B. My tablecloth? Thank you very much.
5. A. I really like your teapot.
   B. My teapot? Thank you very much.
6. A. I really like your sugar bowl.
   B. My sugar bowl? Thank you very much.

Answers
1. butter dish
2. pitcher
3. salt shaker
4. tablecloth
5. teapot
6. sugar bowl

D. WHAT IS IT?
1. spoon
2. glass
3. mug
4. fork
5. vase
6. bowl

E. WHERE IS IT?
1. table
2. napkin
3. spoon
4. saucer
5. glass
6. plate
7. buffet
8. chandelier

WORKBOOK PAGES 38–39

A. WHAT'S THE WORD?
1. pillow
2. mirror
3. bed
4. blanket
5. dresser
6. blinds

B. MATCHING
1. table
2. clock

3. box
4. frame
5. radio
6. spring

C. WHERE IS IT?
1. bed
2. dresser
3. mattress
4. night table
5. mirror
6. curtains

D. LISTENING
Listen and circle the words you hear.

1. A. Ooh! There's a big bug on the blanket.
   B. On the blanket? I'll get it.
2. A. Ooh! There's a big bug on the dresser.
   B. On the dresser? I'll get it.
3. A. Excuse me. I'm looking for a bedspread.
   B. We have some very nice bedspreads on sale this week.
4. A. Excuse me. I'm looking for a mirror.
   B. We have some very nice mirrors on sale this week.
5. A. Oh, no! I just lost my contact lens! I think it's on the pillow.
   B. On the pillow? I'll help you look.
6. A. I'm looking for a clock radio.
   B. Clock radios are over there.
   A. Thank you.

Answers
1. blanket
2. dresser
3. bedspread
4. mirror
5. pillow
6. clock radio

WORKBOOK PAGE 40

A. WHAT'S IN THE KITCHEN?
1. oven
2. toaster
3. dishwasher
4. sink
5. cabinet
6. stove
7. microwave
8. blender
9. refrigerator

B. MATCHING
1. opener
2. rack
3. pail
4. board
5. kettle
6. rack
7. oven
8. compactor

WORKBOOK PAGE 41

A. WHAT IS IT?
1. crib
2. stroller
3. doll
4. car seat
5. swing
6. high chair

B. MATCHING
1. in the playpen.
2. on the chest.
3. in the toy chest.
4. on the changing table.
5. over the crib.

WORKBOOK PAGE 42

A. WHAT'S IN THE BATHROOM?
1. mirror
2. toothbrush
3. bathtub
4. sink
5. soap
6. plunger
7. toilet
8. shower
9. bath mat

B. LISTENING
Listen and circle the word you hear.

1. A. Did you clean the mirror?
   B. The mirror? No, not yet.
2. A. Did you clean the sink?
   B. The sink? No, not yet.
3. A. Did you clean the shower?
   B. The shower? No, not yet.
4. A. Did you clean the toilet?
   B. The toilet? No, not yet.
5. A. Did you clean the sponge?
   B. The sponge? No, not yet.
6. A. Did you clean the tub?
   B. The tub? No, not yet.

Answers
1. mirror
2. sink
3. shower
4. toilet
5. sponge
6. tub

WORKBOOK PAGE 43

A. WHAT IS IT?
1. window
2. lamppost
3. garage
4. lawnmower
5. mailbox
6. chimney

B. MATCHING
1. door
2. mailbox
3. satellite dish
4. lawnmower
5. garage

WORKBOOK PAGES 44–45

A. CHOOSE THE CORRECT WORD
1. vacancy sign
2. lease
3. key
4. fire escape
5. air conditioner
6. trash bin

B. MATCHING
1. truck
2. garage
3. manager
4. pool
5. conditioner
6. deposit

C. WHAT IS IT?
1. mailbox
2. stairway
3. elevator
4. fire alarm
5. smoke detector
6. laundry room

D. MATCHING
1. detector
2. exit
3. chute
4. lock
5. system
6. room

WORKBOOK PAGES 46–47

A. WHO IS IT?
1. painter
2. carpenter
3. locksmith
4. roofer
5. plumber
6. electrician

B. MATCHING: *Who Repairs It?*
1. roofer
2. plumber
3. carpenter
4. electrician
5. locksmith

C. WHAT ARE THEY?
1. ants   2. mice   3. bees   4. rats

D. MATCHING: *Household Problems*
1. leaking.
2. peeling.
3. open.
4. ring.
5. working.

E. MATCHING: *What's the Problem? Who Should You Call?*

1. Call an electrician.
2. Call a plumber.
3. Call an exterminator.
4. Call an appliance repairperson.
5. Call a chimneysweep.

WORKBOOK PAGE 48

A. WHAT IS IT?

1. mop	6. vacuum
2. dustpan	7. scrub brush
3. bucket	8. paper towels
4. broom	9. window cleaner
5. sponge	

B. MATCHING: *What Do You Use?*

1. mop	4. ammonia
2. broom	5. cleanser
3. dust cloth	6. trash can

WORKBOOK PAGE 49

A. WHAT IS IT?

1. paint	6. sandpaper
2. plunger	7. bug spray
3. paintbrush	8. fly swatter
4. fuses	9. tape measure
5. batteries	

B. WHERE ARE THEY?

1. yardstick	4. mousetrap
2. glue	5. paint pan
3. batteries	6. flashlight

WORKBOOK PAGE 50

A. WHAT IS IT?

1. saw	6. pliers
2. hammer	7. nail
3. ax	8. screw
4. wrench	9. screwdriver
5. toolbox	

B. MATCHING

1. saw	4. drill
2. screwdriver	5. stripper
3. wrench	

WORKBOOK PAGE 51

A. WHAT IS IT?

1. rake	6. lawnmower
2. hose	7. trowel
3. nozzle	8. weeder
4. shovel	9. sprinkler
5. hoe	

B. WHAT DO YOU USE?

1. rake	4. seeds
2. lawnmower	5. clippers
3. garden hose	6. pruning shears

WORKBOOK PAGES 52–53

A. WHAT'S THE PLACE?

1. bakery	7. coffee shop
2. clinic	8. gas station
3. bank	9. bus station
4. grocery store	10. book store
5. cleaners	11. card store
6. drug store	12. day-care center

B. MATCHING

1. florist
2. service station
3. pharmacy
4. optician
5. day-care center

C. MATCHING

1. electronics store
2. bank
3. barber shop
4. fast-food restaurant
5. gas station

D. LISTENING

Listen and circle the place you hear.

1. A. Where are you going?
   B. To the coffee shop.
   A. The coffee shop?
   B. Yes.
2. A. Where are you going?
   B. To the book store.
   A. The book store?
   B. Yes.
3. A. Where are you going?
   B. To the furniture store.
   A. The furniture store?
   B. Yes.
4. A. Where are you going?
   B. To the computer store.
   A. The computer store?
   B. Yes.
5. A. Where are you going?
   B. To the copy center.
   A. The copy center?
   B. Yes.
6. A. Where are you going?
   B. To the gas station.
   A. The gas station?
   B. Yes.

Answers

1. coffee shop
2. book store
3. furniture store
4. computer store
5. copy center
6. gas station

WORKBOOK PAGES 54–55

A. WHAT'S THE PLACE?

1. park	7. toy store
2. library	8. laundromat
3. school	9. hotel
4. hospital	10. mall
5. restaurant	11. supermarket
6. post office	12. health club

B. MATCHING

1. library	4. restaurant
2. post office	5. toy store
3. school	

C. WORDSEARCH

```
H O S P I T A L S L Y M Z T
T Y C F N Z I L K I M A D E
Q S C L P A R K B Q L T C E
P C F N C Y L P U R G L C D
S H J R S U P E R M A R K E T
S O R Q Y A O J G R V D W C
V O C K H O T E L Y N B R U
R L Q T B S I A M D P H L Z
B O L A U N D R O M A T F X
```

WORKBOOK PAGES 56–57

A. WHAT'S THE WORD?

1. bus	7. meter maid
2. bus stop	8. parking meter
3. taxi	9. sewer
4. taxi driver	10. sidewalk
5. pedestrian	11. traffic light
6. police officer	12. street sign

B. MATCHING

1. station	4. light
2. meter	5. hydrant
3. container	

C. WHICH GROUP?

People	Places
bus driver	bus stop
pedestrian	intersection
police officer	police station
taxi driver	taxi stand

D. YES OR NO?

1. No	3. No	5. No
2. Yes	4. Yes	

WORKBOOK PAGES 58–59

A. WHAT'S THE WORD?

a. boy	d. man
b. girl	e. baby
c. woman	f. senior citizens

B. WHAT'S THE WORD?

a. young	d. heavy
b. middle-aged	e. average weight
c. old	f. slim

C. WHICH GROUP?

Height	Weight	Age
short	heavy	old
tall	thin	young

D. WHAT DO THEY LOOK LIKE?

1. blond	5. curly
2. brown	6. wavy
3. black	7. bald
4. red	8. mustache

WORKBOOK PAGES 60–61

A. WHAT'S THE WORD?

1. new	7. open
2. old	8. closed
3. large	9. clean
4. small	10. dirty
5. empty	11. easy
6. full	12. difficult

B. MATCHING: *Opposites*

1. little	6. narrow
2. slow	7. young
3. light	8. bad
4. low	9. light
5. tight	10. cold

C. WHAT'S THE WORD?

1. cold
2. single
3. narrow
4. plain
5. heavy
6. dull
7. messy
8. wet

WORKBOOK PAGES 62–63

A. LISTENING

Listen. Put a check under the correct picture.

1. A. You look sad.
   B. I am. I'm VERY sad.
2. A. You look cold.
   B. I am. I'm VERY cold.
3. A. You look thirsty.
   B. I am. I'm VERY thirsty.
4. A. You look worried.
   B. I am. I'm VERY worried.
5. A. You look sick.
   B. I am. I'm VERY sick.
6. A. Are you disappointed?
   B. Yes. I'm VERY disappointed.
7. A. Are you happy?
   B. Yes. I'm VERY happy.
8. A. Are you angry?
   B. Yes. I'm VERY angry.
9. A. Are you nervous?
   B. Yes. I'm VERY nervous.
10. A. Are you confused?
    B. Yes. I'm VERY confused.

Answers

1. ___ ✓
2. ✓ ___
3. ✓ ___
4. ___ ✓
5. ___ ✓
6. ___ ✓
7. ✓ ___
8. ✓ ___
9. ___ ✓
10. ___ ✓

B. CHOOSE THE CORRECT WORD

1. proud
2. happy
3. tired
4. upset
5. embarrassed
6. jealous

C. WHAT'S THE WORD?

1. sad
2. sick
3. thirsty
4. cold
5. surprised
6. confused

WORKBOOK PAGE 64

A. WHAT'S THE WORD?

1. lemon
2. apple
3. pear
4. plum
5. lime
6. orange
7. banana
8. peach
9. grapes

B. LISTENING

Listen and circle the fruit you hear.

1. A. Do we have any cherries?
   B. Cherries? Yes.
2. A. Do we have any lemons?
   B. Lemons? Yes.
3. A. Do we have any prunes?
   B. Prunes? Yes.
4. A. Do you like the papaya?
   B. Yes. This papaya is delicious.
5. A. Do you like the grapes?
   B. Yes. These grapes are delicious.
6. A. Do you like the tangerine?
   B. Yes. This tangerine is delicious.

Answers

1. cherries
2. lemons
3. prunes
4. papaya
5. grapes
6. tangerine

WORKBOOK PAGE 65

A. WHAT'S THE WORD?

1. tomato
2. onion
3. carrot
4. corn
5. potato
6. radish
7. lettuce
8. mushroom
9. cucumber

B. MATCHING

1. squash
2. pepper
3. potato
4. bean
5. sprout

WORKBOOK PAGE 66

A. CHOOSE THE CORRECT WORD

1. turkey
2. ground beef
3. lamb chops
4. crabs
5. roast beef
6. shrimp

B. WHAT'S THE WORD?

1. salmon
2. chicken
3. steak
4. ham
5. bacon
6. lobster

C. WHICH GROUP?

Meat	Poultry	Seafood
ribs	duck	haddock
sausages	turkey	trout

WORKBOOK PAGE 67

A. WHAT'S THE WORD?

1. milk
2. cheese
3. soda
4. butter
5. eggs
6. coffee
7. tofu
8. yogurt
9. cocoa
10. orange juice
11. cottage cheese

B. WHICH GROUP?

Dairy Products	Juices
butter	apple juice
margarine	fruit punch

Beverages
bottled water
diet soda

WORKBOOK PAGE 68

A. WHAT'S THE WORD?

1. salami
2. popcorn
3. nuts
4. frozen lemonade
5. Swiss cheese
6. potato salad

B. LISTENING: *Which Food?*

Listen and put a check under the correct picture.

1. A. May I help you?
   B. Yes, please. I'd like some salami.
2. A. May I help you?
   B. Yes, please. I'd like some roast beef.
3. A. May I help you?
   B. Yes, please. I'd like some American cheese.
4. A. Let's get some potato salad.
   B. Good idea.
5. A. Should we get some frozen dinners?
   B. Yes. Good idea.
6. A. Excuse me. Where are pretzels?
   B. They're in the Snack Foods section.

Answers

1. ✓ ___
2. ___ ✓
3. ___ ✓
4. ✓ ___
5. ✓ ___
6. ___ ✓

C. WHICH GROUP?

Frozen Foods	Snack Foods
frozen lemonade	popcorn
ice cream	pretzels

Deli
corned beef
salami

WORKBOOK PAGE 69

A. WHAT'S THE WORD?

1. ketchup
2. rice
3. bread
4. jelly
5. mayonnaise
6. salsa
7. cereal
8. cookies
9. spaghetti
10. salt
11. soup
12. flour

B. WHICH GROUP?

Packaged Goods	Condiments
cereal	mustard
noodles	pickles

Baked Goods
bread
rolls

WORKBOOK PAGE 70

A. WHAT'S THE WORD?

1. soap
2. napkins
3. diapers
4. formula
5. wipes
6. tissues
7. cat food
8. baby food
9. dog food
10. paper towels
11. toilet paper
12. sandwich bags

B. WHICH GROUP?

Paper Products	Baby Products
napkins	diapers
tissues	formula

Household Items
plastic wrap
soap

WORKBOOK PAGE 71

A. CHOOSE THE CORRECT WORD

1. cashier
2. aisle
3. packer
4. cash register
5. paper bag
6. scale
7. shopping cart
8. shopping basket
9. clerk

B. WHICH GROUP?

People	Things
bagger	counter
cashier	paper bag
manager	scale
shopper	scanner

WORKBOOK PAGES 72–73

A. WHAT'S THE WORD?

1. dozen
2. can
3. bag
4. jar
5. head
6. bunch
7. box
8. pound
9. loaf
10. container
11. quart
12. pint
13. gallon
14. bottle

B. MATCHING

1. baby food
2. cereal
3. soda
4. bananas
5. tuna fish
6. eggs
7. paper towels
8. cabbage

C. WORDSEARCH

WORKBOOK PAGE 74

A. MATCHING

1. tablespoon
2. pint
3. gallon
4. pound
5. ounce
6. teaspoon
7. fluid ounce

B. WHAT'S THE NUMBER?

1. 8
2. 128
3. 1
4. 32
5. 16
6. 8

C. LISTENING

Listen and circle the amount you hear.

1. A. How much milk should I put in?
   B. The recipe says to add one ounce.
   A. One ounce?
   B. Yes.
2. A. How much water should I put in?
   B. The recipe says to add one teaspoon.
   A. One teaspoon?
   B. Yes.
3. A. How much flour should I put in?
   B. The recipe says to add one pound of flour.
   A. One pound?
   B. Yes.
4. A. How much roast beef would you like?
   B. Eight ounces, please.
   A. Eight ounces?
   B. Yes, please.
5. A. How much cheese would you like?
   B. Three quarters of a pound, please.
   A. Three quarters of a pound?
   B. Yes.

6. A. How much milk should I put in?
   B. A cup.
   A. A cup?
   B. Yes. A cup.

Answers

1. ounce
2. tsp.
3. lb.
4. 8 ozs.
5. 3/4 lb.
6. cup

WORKBOOK PAGE 75

A. CHOOSE THE CORRECT WORD

1. slice
2. bake
3. grate
4. fry
5. pour
6. beat

B. MATCHING

1. Chop the onions.
2. Roast the turkey.
3. Peel the orange.
4. Boil the eggs.
5. Stir-fry the vegetables.

WORKBOOK PAGE 76

A. WHAT IS IT?

1. grater
2. pot
3. wok
4. ladle
5. saucepan
6. whisk
7. strainer
8. spatula
9. cake pan

B. MATCHING

1. plate
2. bowl
3. pin
4. opener
5. pan
6. peeler
7. beater
8. knife
9. cutter
10. scoop

WORKBOOK PAGE 77

A. WHAT'S THE WORD?

1. taco
2. salad
3. pizza
4. soda
5. nachos
6. hamburger
7. milkshake
8. hot dog
9. ice cream

B. WHICH GROUP?

Restaurant Supplies	Fast Food
lid	burrito
napkin	milkshake
straw	salad
utensil	taco

C. LISTENING

Listen. Write the number under the correct picture.

1. A. May I help you?
   B. Yes. I'd like a cheeseburger, please.
   A. A cheeseburger?
   B. Yes.
2. A. May I help you?
   B. Yes. I'd like a slice of pizza, please.
   A. A slice of pizza?
   B. Yes.
3. A. May I help you?
   B. Yes. I'd like a hot dog, please.
   A. A hot dog?
   B. Yes.
4. A. May I help you?
   B. Yes. I'd like an order of fried chicken, please.

A. An order of fried chicken?
B. Yes.
5. A. May I help you?
   B. Yes. I'd like a bowl of chili, please.
   A. A bowl of chili?
   B. Yes.
6. A. May I help you?
   B. Yes. I'd like an order of french fries, please.
   A. An order of french fries?
   B. Yes.

Answers

3 5 1 6 4 2

WORKBOOK PAGE 78

A. WHAT'S THE WORD?

1. donut
2. bagel
3. muffin
4. tea
5. coffee
6. pancakes
7. waffles
8. lemonade
9. toast

B. WHICH GROUP?

eat	drink
biscuit	coffee
donut	lemonade
pastry	milk
sandwich	tea

C. LISTENING

Listen. Write the number under the correct picture.

1. A. May I help you?
   B. Yes. I'd like a muffin, please.
   A. A muffin?
   B. Yes.
2. A. May I help you?
   B. Yes. I'd like a tuna fish sandwich, please.
   A. A tuna fish sandwich?
   B. Yes.
3. A. I'd like an order of pancakes, please.
   B. An order of pancakes?
   A. Yes.
4. A. I'll have a medium-size iced tea, please.
   B. A medium-size iced tea?
   A. Yes.
5. A. I'd like a bagel, please.
   B. A bagel?
   A. Yes.
6. A. Anything to drink?
   B. Yes. I'll have a small lemonade.
   A. A small lemonade?
   B. Yes.

Answers

2 4 1 6 3 5

WORKBOOK PAGE 79

A. WHAT'S THE WORD?

1. booth
2. waitress
3. dishwasher
4. menu
5. chef
6. high chair
7. waiter
8. table
9. check

B. LISTENING

Listen. Write the number under the correct picture.

1. A. Do you have any job openings?
   B. Yes. We're looking for a busperson.
   A. A busperson?
   B. Yes.

2. A. Do you have any job openings?
   B. Yes. We're looking for a waitress.
   A. A waitress?
   B. Yes.

3. A. Do you have any job openings?
   B. Yes. We're looking for a dishwasher.
   A. A dishwasher?
   B. Yes.

4. A. Do you have any job openings?
   B. Yes. We're looking for a host or hostess.
   A. A host or hostess?
   B. Yes.

5. A. Do you have any job openings?
   B. Yes. We're looking for a chef.
   A. A chef?
   B. Yes.

6. A. Do you have any job openings?
   B. Yes. We're looking for a waiter.
   A. A waiter?
   B. Yes.

Answers

5 2 6 1 4 3

WORKBOOK PAGE 80

A. CHOOSE THE CORRECT WORD

1. cake	4. potato skins
2. nachos	5. salad
3. jello	6. baked potato

B. WHAT'S ON THE MENU?

Appetizers
nachos
fruit cup

Salads
antipasto
spinach salad

Side Dishes
rice
mashed potatoes

Entrees
meatloaf
roast beef
spaghetti
broiled fish
baked chicken

Desserts
jello
pudding

WORKBOOK PAGE 81

A. WHAT'S THE COLOR?

1. red	6. white
2. blue	7. black
3. pink	8. yellow
4. brown	9. orange
5. green	

B. CROSSWORD

(See page 188.)

WORKBOOK PAGE 82

A. WHAT'S THE WORD?

1. shirt	6. suit
2. pants	7. dress
3. blouse	8. shorts
4. jacket	9. sweater
5. skirt	

B. LISTENING

Listen and circle the word you hear.

1. A. Do you like my new blouse?
   B. Yes. It's a very nice blouse.

2. A. Do you like my new jacket?
   B. Yes. It's a very nice jacket.

3. A. Do you like my new shirt?
   B. Yes. It's a very nice shirt.

4. A. Do you like my new tie?
   B. Yes. It's a very nice tie.

5. A. Do you like my new suit?
   B. Yes. It's a very nice suit.

6. A. Do you like my new skirt?
   B. Yes. It's a very nice skirt.

Answers

1. blouse	4. tie
2. jacket	5. suit
3. shirt	6. skirt

WORKBOOK PAGE 83

A. WHAT'S THE WORD?

1. cap	6. gloves
2. jacket	7. coat
3. hat	8. mittens
4. poncho	9. sunglasses
5. raincoat	

B. WHICH GROUP?

It's raining!
poncho
raincoat
umbrella

It's cold!
gloves
overcoat
ski hat

WORKBOOK PAGE 84

A. WHAT'S THE WORD?

1. stockings	6. nightgown
2. pajamas	7. knee socks
3. socks	8. boxer shorts
4. slippers	9. long underwear
5. bathrobe	

B. WHICH GROUP?

Sleepwear
nightgown
nightshirt
pajamas

Underwear
briefs
slip
stockings

WORKBOOK PAGE 85

A. WHAT'S THE WORD?

1. swimsuit	6. shoes
2. sneakers	7. sandals
3. boots	8. sweatpants
4. sweatshirt	9. flip-flops
5. T-shirt	

B. WHICH GROUP?

Exercise Clothing
leotard
swimsuit
T-shirt

Footwear
boots
sandals
shoes

WORKBOOK PAGE 86

A. CHOOSE THE CORRECT WORD

1. necklace	4. watch
2. earrings	5. backpack
3. ring	6. change purse

B. MATCHING

1. ring	4. bag
2. watch	5. links
3. purse	6. necklace

WORKBOOK PAGE 87

A. CHOOSE THE CORRECT WORD

1. short-sleeved
2. ankle socks
3. turtleneck
4. cardigan sweater
5. striped
6. polka-dotted

B. LISTENING

Listen. Put a check under the correct picture.

1. A. May I help you?
   B. Yes, please. I'm looking for pierced earrings.
   A. Pierced earrings?
   B. Yes.

2. A. What kind of shirt are you looking for?
   B. I'm looking for a plaid shirt.
   A. A plaid shirt?
   B. Yes.

3. A. May I help you?
   B. Yes. I'm looking for a turtleneck shirt.
   A. A turtleneck shirt?
   B. Yes.

4. A. How do you like this short-sleeved shirt?
   B. It's very nice.

5. A. How do you like this blue and white striped shirt?
   B. It's very nice.

6. A. May I help you?
   B. Yes, please. I'm looking for a polka-dotted blouse.

Answers

1.	___	✓
2.	___	✓
3.	✓	___
4.	___	✓
5.	✓	___
6.	___	✓

WORKBOOK PAGE 88

A. WHAT'S THE WORD?

1. small	7. short
2. large	8. long
3. tight	9. wide
4. loose	10. narrow
5. light	11. low
6. heavy	12. high

B. MATCHING: *Opposites*

1. short	6. tight
2. light	7. big
3. baggy	8. low
4. plain	9. lengthen
5. narrow	10. let out

WORKBOOK PAGE 89

A. WHAT'S THE WORD?
1. iron
2. dryer
3. bleach
4. hanger
5. washer
6. clothespin
7. laundry
8. closet
9. clothesline

B. MATCHING
1. starch
2. detergent
3. board
4. softener
5. remover
6. trap

WORKBOOK PAGE 90

A. WHICH DEPARTMENT?
1. Furniture
2. Jewelry
3. Men's Clothing
4. Household Appliances
5. Housewares
6. Women's Clothing
7. Electronics

B. MATCHING
1. bar
2. room
3. fountain
4. department
5. counter

WORKBOOK PAGE 91

A. LABEL INFORMATION
1. 100% cotton
2. Small
3. $40.00
4. 30% off
5. $28.00
6. Wash in Cold Water

B. MATCHING: *A Store Receipt*
1. $18.00
2. 40% off
3. $30.00
4. $18.90
5. $.90

WORKBOOK PAGE 92

A. WHAT'S THE WORD?
a. TV
b. camcorder
c. radio
d. headphones
e. stereo system
f. speaker
g. DVD player
h. clock radio

B. MATCHING
1. radio
2. recorder
3. system
4. player
5. control

WORKBOOK PAGE 93

A. WHAT'S THE WORD?
a. telephone
b. pager
c. cell phone
d. cordless phone
e. answering machine
f. camera
g. zoom lens
h. camera case
i. tripod
j. flash attachment

B. MATCHING
1. camera
2. phone
3. machine
4. lens
5. charger

WORKBOOK PAGE 94

A. WHAT'S THE WORD?
a. computer
b. CD-ROM
c. monitor
d. cable
e. keyboard
f. mouse
g. computer game
h. printer

B. MATCHING
1. computer
2. drive
3. protector
4. screen
5. program

WORKBOOK PAGE 95

A. WHAT'S THE WORD?
a. blocks
b. toy truck
c. doll
d. doll house
e. crayons
f. coloring book
g. wagon
h. swing set
i. bicycle
j. jump rope
k. tricycle
l. skateboard

WORKBOOK PAGE 96

A. CHOOSE THE CORRECT WORD
1. check
2. credit card
3. deposit slip
4. traveler's check
5. teller
6. security guard

B. AT THE BANK
(See page 188.)

WORKBOOK PAGE 97

A. WHAT'S THE WORD?
1. bill
2. check
3. checkbook
4. cash
5. ATM card
6. money order

B. USING AN ATM MACHINE
2 5 1 4 6 3

C. PAY THE BILL
(See page 188.)

WORKBOOK PAGE 98

A. WHAT'S THE WORD?
1. envelope
2. postcard
3. stamp
4. letter
5. package
6. mailbox
7. air letter
8. zip code
9. money order

B. MATCHING
1. carrier
2. address
3. letter
4. order
5. post
6. code

WORKBOOK PAGE 99

A. WHAT'S THE WORD?
1. librarian
2. checkout desk
3. atlas
4. encyclopedia
5. shelves
6. online catalog
7. newspaper
8. magazine

B. WHICH SECTION OF THE LIBRARY?

Reference Section
dictionary
encyclopedia

Periodical Section
newspaper
magazine

Media Section
audiotape
DVD

WORKBOOK PAGE 100

A. WHAT'S THE WORD?
1. firefighter
2. fire engine
3. EMT
4. ambulance
5. mayor
6. city hall
7. sanitation worker
8. recycling center

B. MATCHING: *Where Do They Work?*
1. police station
2. city hall
3. dump
4. child-care center
5. senior center

WORKBOOK PAGE 101

A. WHAT'S THE WORD?
a. burglary
b. mugging
c. vandalism
d. robbery
e. car accident
f. downed power line
g. fire
h. water main break

B. MATCHING
1. accident
2. outage
3. child
4. break
5. spill

WORKBOOK PAGES 102–103

A. WHAT IS IT?
a. head
b. hair
c. eye
d. ear
e. nose
f. mouth
g. teeth
h. chin
i. neck
j. shoulder
k. chest
l. back
m. arm
n. elbow
o. waist
p. leg

B. WHAT IS IT?
a. hand
b. finger
c. thumb
d. foot
e. ankle
f. toe

C. MATCHING: *Where Are They?*
1. neck
2. hand
3. foot
4. mouth
5. head
6. arm

D. HOW MANY DO WE HAVE?
1. 2
2. 10
3. 1
4. 2
5. 1
6. 10
7. 1
8. 2
9. 1
10. 2

WORKBOOK PAGES 104–105

A. CHOOSE THE CORRECT WORD
1. headache
2. stomachache
3. fever
4. insect bite
5. toothache
6. cough
7. cold
8. stiff neck
9. the chills

B. LISTENING
Listen and circle the word you hear.

1. A. What's the matter?
   B. I have a headache.
   A. A headache? I'm sorry to hear that.

2. A. What's the matter?
   B. I have a cold.
   A. A cold? I'm sorry to hear that.

3. A. What's the matter?
   B. I have a stomachache.
   A. A stomachache? I'm sorry to hear that.
4. A. What's the matter?
   B. I have a bloody nose.
   A. A bloody nose? I'm sorry to hear that.
5. A. What's the matter?
   B. I have a fever.
   A. A fever? I'm sorry to hear that.
6. A. What's the matter?
   B. I have the hiccups.
   A. The hiccups? I'm sorry to hear that.

Answers

1. headache	4. bloody nose
2. cold	5. fever
3. stomachache	6. hiccups

C. CHOOSE THE CORRECT WORD

1. dizzy	4. exhausted
2. cut	5. cough
3. burn	6. sneeze

D. WORDSEARCH

```
V F D H R B M P C D I E G H
Q D I V E R M D O O R M S F
C Q Z I S L F W L P G N N E
U L Z U V H E A D A C H E V
A U Y R A C V L I Q H U E E
T E R W A P E E P A S D Z W
P S U N B U R N O G R C E Q
Z F N O P W R G S Q E X H B
```

WORKBOOK PAGE 106

A. WHAT'S THE WORD?

1. bandage	4. aspirin
2. gauze	5. splint
3. tweezers	6. sterile pad

B. MATCHING: *First-Aid Supplies*

1. kit	4. peroxide
2. tape	5. pain reliever
3. ointment	

C. MATCHING: *First-Aid Procedures*

1. rescue breathing
2. Heimlich maneuver
3. splint
4. tourniquet
5. CPR

WORKBOOK PAGE 107

A. CHOOSE THE CORRECT WORD

1. heatstroke	6. unconscious
2. the flu	7. chicken pox
3. measles	8. in shock
4. heart attack	9. frostbite
5. asthma	

B. MATCHING

1. throat	4. infection
2. pressure	5. pox
3. disease	

WORKBOOK PAGE 108

A. WHAT'S THE WORD?

1. scale	4. needle
2. thermometer	5. eye chart
3. stethoscope	6. X-ray machine

B. MATCHING: *In the Doctor's Office*

1. eyes	4. heart
2. weight	5. blood
3. temperature	

C. MATCHING: *What Did the Doctor Do?*

1. my temperature.	4. my height.
2. my heart.	5. some blood.
3. my ears.	

WORKBOOK PAGE 109

A. CHOOSE THE CORRECT WORD

1. doctor	6. sling
2. nurse	7. crutches
3. stitches	8. prescription
4. cast	9. wound
5. injection	

B. MATCHING

1. form	3. hygienist	5. pack
2. room	4. ball	

WORKBOOK PAGE 110

A. CHOOSE THE CORRECT WORD

1. gargle	6. walker
2. exercise	7. heating pad
3. acupuncture	8. blood work
4. air purifier	9. counseling
5. braces	

B. MATCHING

1. fluids	4. a diet
2. bed	5. a specialist
3. vitamins	

WORKBOOK PAGE 111

A. CHOOSE THE CORRECT WORD

1. aspirin	6. cream
2. eye drops	7. capsule
3. vitamins	8. pill
4. antacid tablets	9. tablespoon
5. cold tablets	

B. MATCHING

1. syrup	4. drops
2. lozenges	5. tablets
3. spray	

WORKBOOK PAGE 112

A. CHOOSE THE CORRECT WORD

1. pediatrician	6. orthodontist
2. allergist	7. cardiologist
3. orthopedist	8. ophthalmologist
4. audiologist	9. physical therapist
5. chiropractor	

B. MATCHING

1. ophthalmologist
2. cardiologist
3. audiologist
4. gastroenterologist
5. orthodontist

WORKBOOK PAGE 113

A. CHOOSE THE CORRECT WORD

1. hospital bed	6. I.V.
2. X-ray technician	7. surgeon
3. operating room	8. laboratory
4. obstetrician	9. gurney
5. medical chart	

B. MATCHING

1. chart	4. button
2. gown	5. monitor
3. pan	

WORKBOOK PAGE 114

A. WHAT IS IT?

1. comb	4. shampoo
2. razor	5. scissors
3. toothbrush	6. hair brush

B. WHICH GROUP?

For teeth	For hair	For the face
dental floss	brush	blush
mouthwash	comb	eyeliner
toothbrush	conditioner	lipstick
toothpaste	shampoo	mascara

C. LISTENING

Listen. Write the correct number.

1. A. Excuse me. I'm looking for a hair brush.
   B. Hair brushes are in the next aisle.
   A. Thank you.
2. A. Excuse me. Where can I find shampoo?
   B. It's in the next aisle.
   A. Thank you.
3. A. Excuse me. I'm looking for a comb.
   B. Combs are in the next aisle.
   A. Thanks.
4. A. Where can I find powder?
   B. Powder is in aisle three.
   A. Thank you.
5. A. May I help you?
   B. Yes. I'm looking for toothpaste.
   A. Toothpaste is in aisle two.
   B. Thanks.
6. A. Excuse me. Where can I find scissors?
   B. Scissors? They're in the next aisle.
   A. Thank you.

Answers

3	6	2
4	1	5

WORKBOOK PAGE 115

A. WHAT IS IT?

1. ointment	4. nipple
2. bib	5. pacifier
3. bottle	6. baby food

B. MATCHING

1. powder	4. swabs
2. pins	5. diapers
3. ring	

C. LISTENING

Listen. Write the number under the correct picture.

1. A. Where's the ointment?
   B. The ointment? It's on the changing table.
2. A. Where are the baby wipes?
   B. The baby wipes? They're on the changing table.
3. A. Where are the diaper pins?
   B. The diaper pins? They're on the changing table.
4. A. Where's the pacifier?
   B. The pacifier? It's in the crib.
5. A. Where's the bib?
   B. The bib? It's in the kitchen.
6. A. Where's the baby shampoo?
   B. The baby shampoo? It's on the changing table.

Answers

2   6   1   4   3   5

WORKBOOK PAGE 116

A. CHOOSE THE CORRECT WORD

1. college
2. middle school
3. trade school
4. adult school
5. preschool
6. medical school

B. WHAT'S THE ORDER?

4	3
6	5
1	2

C. MATCHING

1. preschool
2. high school
3. elementary school
4. adult school
5. middle school

WORKBOOK PAGE 117

A. WHERE ARE THEY?

1. principal, office
2. coach, gym
3. custodian, cafeteria
4. nurse, nurse's office
5. teacher, science lab
6. guidance counselor, guidance office

WORKBOOK PAGE 118

A. WHAT'S THE SUBJECT?

1. health
2. math
3. art
4. history
5. science
6. music
7. French
8. chemistry
9. geography

B. WHICH GROUP?

Social Studies	Languages
geography	French
history	Spanish

Science
biology
chemistry

WORKBOOK PAGE 119

A. WHAT'S THE ACTIVITY?

1. choir
2. band
3. football
4. drama
5. orchestra
6. pep squad
7. school newspaper
8. community service
9. student government

B. WHICH GROUP?

Music	Clubs	Writing
band	chess	newspaper
orchestra	debate	yearbook

WORKBOOK PAGES 120–121

A. MATCHING

1. multiplication
2. subtraction
3. division
4. addition

B. MATCHING

1. −
2. ×
3. =
4. +
5. ÷

C. LISTENING

Listen and circle the answer.

1. A. How much is three times two?
   B. Three times two equals six.
2. A. How much is four plus five?
   B. Four plus five equals nine.
3. A. How much is nine divided by three?
   B. Nine divided by three equals three.
4. A. How much is eight minus two?
   B. Eight minus two equals six.
5. A. How much is two times five?
   B. Two times five equals ten.

Answers

1. ×
2. +
3. ÷
4. −
5. ×

D. WRITE THE MATH PROBLEMS

1. $1 + 6 = 7$
2. $8 \div 4 = 2$
3. $2 \times 5 = 10$
4. $12 - 7 = 5$

E. WHAT'S THE FRACTION?

1/4   1/2   1/3   2/3   3/4

F. MATCHING

1. 1/2
2. 1/4
3. 2/3
4. 3/4
5. 1/3

G. LISTENING

Listen and circle the answer.

1. A. Is this on sale?
   B. Yes. It's one third off the regular price.
   A. One third off the regular price?
   B. That's right.
2. A. Is this on sale?
   B. Yes. It's one half off the regular price.
   A. One half off the regular price?
   B. That's right.
3. A. Is this on sale?
   B. Yes. It's one quarter off the regular price.
   A. One quarter off the regular price?
   B. That's right.
4. A. The gas tank is three quarters full.
   B. Three quarters?
   A. Yes.
5. A. The gas tank is half full.
   B. Half full?
   A. Yes.

Answers

1. 1/3
2. 1/2
3. 1/4
4. 3/4
5. 1/2

H. WHAT'S THE PERCENT?

25%   75%   50%   100%

I. MATCHING

1. 50%
2. 25%
3. 100%
4. 30%
5. 75%

J. LISTENING

Listen and write the percent you hear.

1. A. There's a fifty percent chance of rain.
   B. Fifty percent?
   A. Yes.
2. A. There's a one hundred percent chance of rain.
   B. One hundred percent?
   A. Yes.
3. A. How did you do on the test?
   B. I got ninety percent of the answers right.
   A. Ninety percent?
   B. Yes.
4. A. How did you do on the test?
   B. I got seventy-five percent of the answers right.
   A. Seventy-five percent?
   B. Yes.
5. A. Is this on sale?
   B. Yes. It's twenty-five percent off the regular price.
   A. Twenty-five percent?
   B. Yes. That's right.
6. A. Is this on sale?
   B. Yes. It's ten percent off the regular price.
   A. Ten percent?
   B. Yes. That's right.

Answers

1. 50%
2. 100%
3. 90%
4. 75%
5. 25%
6. 10%

WORKBOOK PAGES 122–123

A. WHAT'S THE WORD?

1. circle
2. square
3. line
4. triangle
5. rectangle
6. cube
7. cylinder
8. cone
9. pyramid
10. angle
11. sphere
12. ellipse

B. WHICH GROUP?

Triangle	Circle
base	diameter
hypotenuse	radius

Rectangle	
length	
width	

C. WHAT'S THE WORD?

a. inch	d. centimeter
b. foot	e. meter
c. yard	

D. MATCHING: *Abbreviations*

1. centimeter	5. inch
2. meter	6. foot
3. mile	7. yard
4. kilometer	

E. WHAT'S THE ANSWER?

1. 1"	4. 1 mi.
2. 12"	5. 3'
3. 1 yd.	6. 1'

WORKBOOK PAGES 124–125

A. WHAT'S THE PART OF SPEECH?

1. f	5. d
2. c	6. a
3. e	7. b
4. g	

B. MATCHING: *Types of Sentences*

1. imperative	3. exclamatory
2. interrogative	4. declarative

C. MATCHING: *Parts of Speech*

1. verb	5. verb
2. adjective	6. preposition
3. article	7. noun
4. noun	8. pronoun

D. MATCHING: *Punctuation Marks*

1. period
2. comma
3. question mark
4. quotation marks
5. apostrophe
6. exclamation point
7. colon
8. semi-colon

E. FIX THE SENTENCES

1. My sister's name is Berta.
2. What's your telephone number?
3. These cookies are fantastic!
4. Please get milk, eggs, and bread at the supermarket.
5. My children are in elementary school.
6. Our school has three music activities: the band, the orchestra, and the choir.

F. THE WRITING PROCESS

1. ideas	4. feedback
2. draft	5. final
3. corrections	

WORKBOOK PAGE 126

A. CHOOSE THE CORRECT WORD

1. biography	4. postcard
2. editorial	5. note
3. invitation	6. letter

B. MATCHING

1. thank-you note
2. autobiography
3. postcard
4. invitation
5. instant message
6. editorial

C. WHICH GROUP?

Fiction	Non-Fiction
novel	autobiography
short story	biography

Mail	
letter	
postcard	

WORKBOOK PAGE 127

A. WHAT'S THE WORD?

a. forest	d. waterfall
b. hill	e. river
c. lake	f. rainforest

B. WHAT IS IT?

1. river	4. lake
2. island	5. canyon
3. desert	6. peninsula

C. WHICH GROUP?

Land	Water
desert	lake
meadow	ocean
mountain	pond
plains	river

WORKBOOK PAGE 128

A. WHAT'S THE WORD?

1. flask	6. microscope
2. scale	7. dropper
3. prism	8. funnel
4. magnet	9. test tube
5. beaker	

B. MATCHING

1. tongs	4. cylinder
2. dish	5. method
3. burner	

WORKBOOK PAGE 129

A. WHAT'S THE WORD?

1. moon	5. comet
2. sun	6. Earth
3. star	7. telescope
4. satellite	8. astronaut

B. WHAT'S MISSING?

1. Mars	4. Jupiter
2. Earth	5. Neptune
3. Venus	6. Mercury

C. MATCHING

1. Dipper	4. station
2. eclipse	5. saucer
3. moon	

WORKBOOK PAGES 130–131

A. WHAT'S THE OCCUPATION?

1. chef	7. engineer
2. baker	8. custodian
3. farmer	9. hairdresser
4. cashier	10. accountant
5. assembler	11. architect
6. carpenter	12. firefighter

B. MATCHING: *What's the Job?*

1. worker	4. clerk
2. person	5. representative
3. aide	

C. MATCHING: *Who Uses It?*

1. custodian	5. cashier
2. carpenter	6. gardener
3. chef	7. barber
4. artist	8. accountant

WORKBOOK PAGES 132–133

A. WHAT'S THE OCCUPATION?

1. mover	7. painter
2. teacher	8. secretary
3. salesperson	9. translator
4. mechanic	10. waiter
5. welder	11. waitress
6. pharmacist	12. lawyer

B. MATCHING: *Who Works There?*

1. pharmacist	4. waiter
2. secretary	5. salesperson
3. teacher	6. mechanic

C. CROSSWORD

(See page 188.)

WORKBOOK PAGES 134–135

A. WHAT DO THEY DO?

1. sew	7. paint
2. cook	8. serve
3. file	9. clean
4. sell	10. drive
5. wash	11. deliver
6. type	12. assemble

B. MATCHING

1. drive.
2. act.
3. bake.
4. paint.
5. assemble components.
6. build things.
7. clean.

C. MATCHING

1. buildings.	4. an airplane.
2. food.	5. the piano.
3. lawns.	6. cars.

WORKBOOK PAGE 136

A. CHOOSE THE CORRECT WORD

1. sign	4. application
2. classified ad	5. interview
3. job notice	6. benefits

B. MATCHING: *Abbreviations*

1. hour
2. evenings
3. full-time
4. part-time
5. previous
6. required
7. experience
8. available
9. Monday through Friday
10. excellent

A. WHAT'S THE WORD?
a. coat rack
b. message board
c. copier
d. cubicle
e. file cabinet
f. file clerk
g. coffee machine
h. water cooler

B. MATCHING
1. area
2. board
3. cabinet
4. lounge
5. machine

WORKBOOK PAGE 138

A. WHAT IS IT?
1. desk
2. glue
3. thumbtack
4. envelope
5. index card
6. paper clip
7. stapler
8. clipboard
9. rubber band

B. MATCHING
1. clip
2. pad
3. band
4. folder
5. stick
6. tape

WORKBOOK PAGE 139

A. CHOOSE THE CORRECT WORD
1. time clock
2. suggestion box
3. shipping clerk
4. forklift
5. conveyor belt
6. assembly line
7. loading dock
8. hand truck
9. payroll office

B. MATCHING
1. clock
2. line
3. station
4. box
5. belt

WORKBOOK PAGE 140

A. WHAT'S THE WORD?
1. crane
2. ladder
3. bulldozer
4. wire
5. backhoe
6. dump truck
7. wood
8. brick
9. wheelbarrow

B. WHICH GROUP?

Materials	Machines
beam	backhoe
pipe	bulldozer
plywood	cement mixer

WORKBOOK PAGE 141

A. WHAT'S THE WORD?
1. helmet
2. mask
3. hairnet
4. first-aid kit
5. back support
6. safety glasses

B. MATCHING
1. head
2. eyes
3. face
4. feet
5. hands

C. LISTENING: *Warnings*

Listen and write the number under the correct picture.

1. A. Don't forget to wear your safety earmuffs!
   B. Thanks for reminding me.
2. A. Be careful! That's poisonous!
   B. Thanks for the warning.
3. A. Watch out! That's flammable!
   B. Thanks for the warning.
4. A. Don't forget to wear your hard hat!
   B. Thanks for reminding me.
5. A. Be careful! That material is corrosive!
   B. Thanks for the warning.
6. A. Be careful! That work area is radioactive!
   B. Thanks for the warning.

Answers

5   3   2   6   1   4

WORKBOOK PAGE 142

A. WHAT'S THE WORD?
1. bus
2. taxi
3. bus station
4. conductor
5. ticket
6. train
7. bus driver
8. bus stop
9. ferry

B. MATCHING
1. counter
2. stop
3. card
4. compartment
5. booth

WORKBOOK PAGE 143

A. WHAT'S THE WORD?
1. sedan
2. jeep
3. motorcycle
4. van
5. bicycle
6. convertible
7. pickup truck
8. moving van
9. tractor trailer

B. MATCHING
1. car
2. scooter
3. wagon
4. trailer
5. truck

WORKBOOK PAGES 144–145

A. WHAT'S THE WORD?
1. tire
2. headlight
3. bumper
4. engine
5. battery
6. radiator
7. flare
8. jack
9. spare tire
10. gas pump
11. nozzle
12. gas cap

B. MATCHING
1. wipers
2. defroster
3. plate
4. plugs
5. belt

C. CHOOSE THE CORRECT WORD
1. seat belt
2. steering wheel
3. accelerator
4. gearshift
5. gas gauge
6. rearview mirror
7. radio
8. oil
9. air bag

D. MATCHING
1. bag
2. belt
3. mirror
4. signal
5. brake

WORKBOOK PAGE 146

A. WHAT'S THE WORD?
1. tollbooth
2. bridge
3. crosswalk
4. exit sign
5. tunnel
6. traffic light
7. route sign
8. highway
9. intersection

B. MATCHING
1. sign
2. lane
3. light
4. highway
5. ramp

WORKBOOK PAGE 147

A. WHAT'S THE WORD?
1. off
2. on
3. down
4. up
5. over
6. under
7. into
8. out of

B. LISTENING: *Following Directions*

Listen and write the number under the correct picture.

1. Walk down this street.
2. Go around the corner.
3. Walk across the street.
4. Go over the bridge.
5. Drive under the bridge.
6. Go past the bank.

Answers

6   2   4
5   3   1

WORKBOOK PAGE 148

A. MATCHING: *What's the Sign?*
1. no right turn
2. no left turn
3. no U-turn
4. right turn only
5. pedestrian crossing
6. slippery when wet
7. school crossing
8. railroad crossing

B. WHAT'S THE COMPASS DIRECTION?

```
        north
west              east
        south
```

C. LISTENING: *Traffic Signs*

Listen and write the number under the correct sign.

1. You have to stop. There's a stop sign.
2. This is handicapped parking only.
3. Don't turn right. The sign says "no right turn".
4. Careful! That sign says "merging traffic".
5. You can't go on that street. Do you see the sign?

Answers

3   1   5   2   4

A. CHOOSE THE CORRECT WORD

1. ticket
2. suitcase
3. customs officer
4. passport
5. boarding pass
6. security officer
7. security checkpoint
8. baggage claim area

B. MATCHING

1. officer
2. checkpoint
3. counter
4. pass
5. detector

A. CHOOSE THE CORRECT WORD

1. cockpit
2. lavatory
3. life vest
4. tray
5. seat belt
6. emergency exit

B. MATCHING

1. exit
2. belt
3. bag
4. attendant
5. compartment
6. mask
7. sign

A. WHAT'S THE WORD?

1. front desk
2. desk clerk
3. bellhop
4. luggage cart
5. housekeeper
6. housekeeping cart
7. doorman
8. parking attendant

B. MATCHING

1. desk
2. shop
3. room
4. key
5. cart

A. CHOOSE THE CORRECT WORD

1. thread
2. chess
3. dice
4. pottery
5. astronomy
6. stamp album
7. binoculars
8. woodworking
9. sewing machine

B. MATCHING

1. photography
2. sewing
3. pottery
4. painting
5. astronomy

A. WHAT'S THE WORD?

1. beach
2. zoo
3. museum
4. concert
5. movies
6. aquarium
7. play
8. carnival
9. mountains

B. MATCHING

1. sale
2. market
3. gallery
4. gardens
5. park

A. WHAT'S THE WORD?

1. bench
2. seesaw
3. ballfield
4. grill
5. slide
6. sandbox
7. trash can
8. bike rack
9. swings

B. MATCHING

1. pond
2. can
3. area
4. fountain
5. path

A. CHOOSE THE CORRECT WORD

1. kite
2. shovel
3. snack bar
4. surfboard
5. shell
6. cooler
7. surfer
8. sun hat
9. lifeguard

B. MATCHING

1. ball
2. lotion
3. preserver
4. stand
5. bar

A. CHOOSE THE CORRECT WORD

1. tent
2. lantern
3. compass
4. sleeping bag
5. backpack
6. thermos

B. WHAT'S THE WORD?

1. bag
2. map
3. stove
4. picnic
5. tent
6. hiking

C. MATCHING

1. stove
2. map
3. bag
4. boots
5. repellent

A. CROSSWORD

(See page 188.)

B. MATCHING

1. bike
2. pong
3. out
4. arts
5. skating

A. WHAT'S THE SPORT?

1. basketball
2. football
3. soccer
4. ice hockey
5. baseball
6. lacrosse

B. WHICH GROUP?

Field	Rink	Court
baseball	ice hockey	basketball
soccer		volleyball

A. WHAT'S THE WORD?

1. basketball
2. backboard
3. baseball
4. bat
5. volleyball
6. volleyball net
7. hockey stick
8. hockey puck

B. LISTENING

Listen. Write the number next to the correct picture.

1. A. I can't find my football helmet.
   B. Your football helmet? Look in the closet.
2. A. I can't find my lacrosse stick.
   B. Your lacrosse stick? Look in the closet.
3. A. Excuse me. I'm looking for a basketball.
   B. Our basketballs are over there.
   A. Thanks.
4. A. Excuse me. I'm looking for a baseball bat.
   B. Our baseball bats are over there.
   A. Thanks.
5. A. I'm going to play hockey after school today.
   B. Don't forget your hockey mask.
6. A. I'm going to play soccer after school today.
   B. Don't forget your shinguards.

Answers

3	6	1
2	4	5

A. CHOOSE THE CORRECT WORD

1. sled
2. ice skates
3. poles
4. snowmobiling
5. snowboarding
6. bobsled
7. saucer
8. downhill skiing

B. MATCHING

1. guards
2. skates
3. dish
4. skiing
5. poles

A. WHAT'S THE WORD?

1. fishing
2. sailing
3. surfing
4. swimming
5. rafting
6. snorkeling
7. canoeing
8. kayaking
9. waterskiing

B. MATCHING

1. fishing
2. snorkeling
3. rowing
4. canoeing
5. swimming
6. surfing

A. CHOOSE THE CORRECT WORD

1. kick
2. stretch
3. reach
4. hit
5. lift
6. dive
7. serve
8. bounce
9. push-up
10. somersault
11. deep knee bend

B. LISTENING

Listen. Write the number under the correct picture.

1. A. Pitch the ball!
   B. Pitch the ball? Okay, Coach!
2. A. Now do a handstand!
   B. A handstand?
   A. Yes.
3. A. Now do a somersault!
   B. A somersault?
   A. Yes.
4. A. Dribble the ball!
   B. Dribble the ball? Okay, Coach.

5. A. Okay, everybody. I want you to do
      twenty push-ups!
   B. Twenty push-ups?!
   A. That's right.
6. A. Okay, everybody. I want you to do
      thirty jumping jacks!
   B. Thirty jumping jacks?!
   A. That's right.

Answers

2   5   4   6   1   3

WORKBOOK PAGE 163

A. WHAT'S THE WORD?

1. actor
2. actress
3. conductor
4. musician
5. ballerina
6. ballet dancer
7. movie theater
8. movie screen

B. MATCHING

1. music club
2. ballet
3. orchestra
4. comedy club
5. play

WORKBOOK PAGE 164

A. CHOOSE THE CORRECT WORD

1. jazz
2. rock music
3. musical
4. cartoon
5. comedy
6. game show

B. LISTENING

*Listen. Write the number next to the
type of music you hear.*

1. (Sound: rap music)
2. (Sound: country)
3. (Sound: jazz)
4. (Sound: classical)
5. (Sound: rock)
6. (Sound: gospel)
7. (Sound: reggae)

Answers

4   3   7   1
6   2   5

WORKBOOK PAGE 165

A. CHOOSE THE CORRECT WORD

1. flute
2. violin
3. piano
4. guitar
5. clarinet
6. tuba

B. WHICH GROUP?

Brass	Strings	Woodwinds
trombone	cello	clarinet
trumpet	violin	flute

C. LISTENING

*Listen. Write the number next to the
instrument you hear.*

1. (Sound: harmonica)
2. (Sound: flute)
3. (Sound: banjo)
4. (Sound: tuba)
5. (Sound: harp)
6. (Sound: drum)

Answers

4   6   2
1   5   3

WORKBOOK PAGE 166

A. WHAT'S THE WORD?

1. farmhouse
2. barn
3. hay
4. field
5. tractor
6. scarecrow
7. farmer
8. cow
9. rooster

B. MATCHING

1. hand
2. pen
3. coop
4. system
5. garden

C. LISTENING

*Listen. Write the number next to the
farm animal you hear.*

1. (Sound: turkey)
2. (Sound: chicken)
3. (Sound: cow)
4. (Sound: goat)
5. (Sound: horse)
6. (Sound: lamb)
7. (Sound: pig)
8. (Sound: rooster)

Answers

5   2   7   1
6   8   3   4

WORKBOOK PAGE 167

A. WHAT'S THE WORD?

1. deer
2. rabbit
3. monkey
4. bear
5. horse
6. fox
7. elephant
8. bat
9. camel
10. mouse
11. skunk
12. squirrel

B. LISTENING

*Listen. Write the number next to the
animal or pet you hear.*

1. (Sound: lion)
2. (Sound: bear)
3. (Sound: mouse)
4. (Sound: hyena)
5. (Sound: donkey)
6. (Sound: dog)
7. (Sound: cat)
8. (Sound: elephant)

Answers

5   2   6   4
3   7   1   8

WORKBOOK PAGE 168

A. WHAT'S THE WORD?

1. bee
2. owl
3. moth
4. ant
5. robin
6. spider
7. eagle
8. parrot

B. WHICH GROUP?

Insects	Birds
fly	swan
moth	crow
spider	pigeon
mosquito	sparrow

C. LISTENING

*Listen. Write the number next to the
bird or insect you hear.*

1. (Sound: cricket)
2. (Sound: crow)
3. (Sound: duck)
4. (Sound: owl)
5. (Sound: bee)
6. (Sound: parrot)
7. (Sound: seagull)
8. (Sound: woodpecker)

Answers

3   4   6   2
7   5   1   8

WORKBOOK PAGE 169

A. WHAT'S THE WORD?

1. seal
2. frog
3. turtle
4. jellyfish
5. whale
6. alligator
7. crab
8. dolphin
9. snake

B. WHICH GROUP?

Fish	Sea Animals	Reptiles
flounder	seal	cobra
tuna	whale	snake

WORKBOOK PAGE 170

A. CHOOSE THE CORRECT WORD

1. trunk
2. flower
3. cone
4. bush
5. tulip
6. cactus
7. vine
8. palm
9. bud

B. WHICH GROUP?

Flowers	Trees
rose	oak
daisy	pine
daffodil	maple
sunflower	redwood

WORKBOOK PAGE 171

A. WHAT'S THE WORD?

1. oil
2. gas
3. wind
4. coal
5. recycle
6. carpool
7. water pollution
8. global warming
9. geothermal energy

B. MATCHING

1. energy
2. warming
3. pollution
4. waste
5. rain

WORKBOOK PAGE 172

A. WHAT'S THE WORD?

1. tornado
2. flood
3. hurricane
4. drought
5. tsunami
6. avalanche
7. wildfire
8. landslide
9. earthquake

B. MATCHING

1. wildfire
2. tsunami
3. blizzard
4. hurricane
5. drought

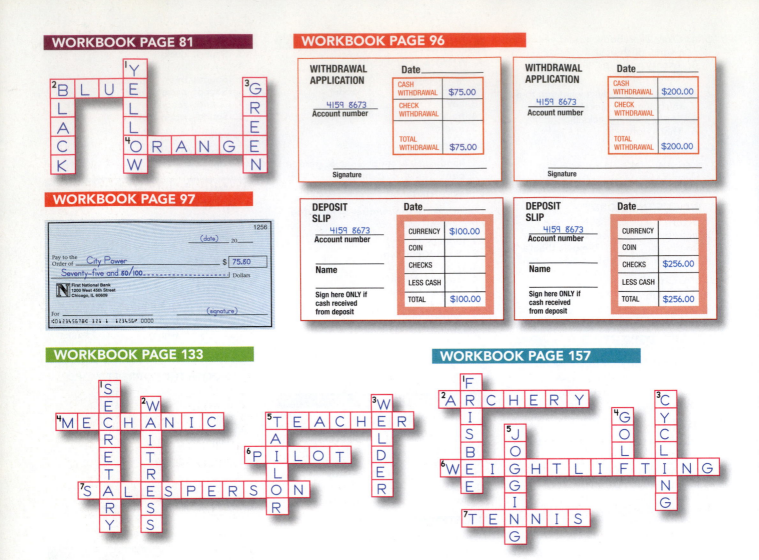

WORKBOOK PAGE 81

¹Y
²B L U E
L   L
A   L
²B L U E   O
C   ⁴O R A N G E
K   W

³G
R
E
E
N

WORKBOOK PAGE 96

WITHDRAWAL APPLICATION

Date _____

4159 8673
Account number

CASH WITHDRAWAL	$75.00
CHECK WITHDRAWAL	
TOTAL WITHDRAWAL	$75.00

_____
Signature

WITHDRAWAL APPLICATION

Date _____

4159 8673
Account number

CASH WITHDRAWAL	$200.00
CHECK WITHDRAWAL	
TOTAL WITHDRAWAL	$200.00

_____
Signature

DEPOSIT SLIP

Date _____

4159 8673
Account number

Name _____

Sign here ONLY if
cash received
from deposit

CURRENCY	$100.00
COIN	
CHECKS	
LESS CASH	
TOTAL	$100.00

DEPOSIT SLIP

Date _____

4159 8673
Account number

Name _____

Sign here ONLY if
cash received
from deposit

CURRENCY	
COIN	
CHECKS	$256.00
LESS CASH	
TOTAL	$256.00

WORKBOOK PAGE 97

1256

(date) ____ 20__

Pay to the
Order of   City Power _____ $ 75.80

Seventy-five and 80/100 --------------------- Dollars

First National Bank
1200 West 45th Street
Chicago, IL 60609

For _____   (signature) _____

⑈012345678⑈ 321 1 123456⑈ 0000

WORKBOOK PAGE 133

¹S
⁴M E C H A N I C   ²W
E   I
C   T   ⁵T E A C H E R   ³W
R   R   A   E
E   E   ⁶P I L O T   L
⁷S A L E S P E R S O N   D
A   S   O   E
R   S   R   R
Y

WORKBOOK PAGE 157

¹F
²A R C H E R Y   ³C
R   ⁴G   Y
I   O   C
S   ⁵J   L   L
⁶W E I G H T L I F T I N G
B   O   N
E   G   G
⁷T E N N I S
G